CELEBRATION OF HAND-HOOKED RUGS XXIV

2014 Edition

Editor
Debra Smith

Author
Ayleen Stellhorn

Designer
CW Design Solutions, Inc.

Advertising Coordinator
Gail Weaverling

Circulation Coordinator
Rebecca Sterner

Magazine Assistant
Candice R. Derr

Operations Manager
Anne Lodge

Publisher
Judith Schnell

Rug photographs provided by the artists unless otherwise noted.

Rug Hooking magazine is published five times a year in Jan./Feb., March/April/May, June/July/Aug., Sept./Oct., and Nov./Dec. by Stackpole, Inc., 5067 Ritter Road, Mechanicsburg, PA 17055. *Celebration of Hand-Hooked Rugs* is published annually. Contents Copyright© 2014. All rights reserved. Reproduction in whole or part without the written consent of the publisher is prohibited. Canadian GST #R137954772.

A Publication of

R·U·G HOOKING

5067 Ritter Road
Mechanicsburg, PA 17055
(717) 796-0411
www.rughookingmagazine.com
rughook@stackpolebooks.com

ISBN-978-0-8117-1441-9

Printed in U.S.A.

WELCOME TO CELEBRATION XXIV

Marti Hertel

The Year of the Canadian

The Celebration rugs are here! It is our pleasure each year to publish this book, filled with the wonderful rugs from the past year's competition. You'll see a wide range of styles and be inspired by the creativity, and I venture to guess that these rugs will elicit more than a few exclamations of "How did she (or he) do that?!"

As the *RHM* staff admires the Celebration entries every fall and winter, we pay attention to geography. We like to know just where these gorgeous rugs are coming from: are they mostly from the Northeast US? Do we have a good showing from the Midwest? How about the Deep South? Since we have gone digital with our entry process, we are getting more rugs from afar. It is just as easy to upload photos of your rug when you are sipping your coffee in British Columbia as it is from just down the road here in Pennsylvania.

I use the example of British Columbia for a reason: I'm calling *Celebration XXIV* the Year of the Canadian. One third of the rugs in this book were entered by and hooked by Canadians. Rugs from Nova Scotia to Alberta and British Columbia and everywhere in between . . . we know that Canada is home to lots of rug hookers, and the book you hold in your hand proves the point. These 23 Canadian rugs showcase the artistry and ingenuity of our rug hooking friends to the north. I hope that this influx of Canadian rugs means that rug hooking is becoming even more popular there. I'm pleased to present these to you and to say unequivocally that this group of Canadian rugs is pretty darn impressive.

Regardless of the geographic origin of the rugs in these pages, you will be moved and inspired by them. It is one of the highlights of our year to bring this publication to you. So turn the page and enjoy the latest edition of *Celebration of Hand-Hooked Rugs*

Debra Smith

Readers' Choice
Remember to vote for your favorite hooked rugs to be a part of the Readers' Choice decision. You can vote either with the paper ballot included in this book or digitally. Go to **www.rughookingmagazine.com** and look for **Celebration Readers' Choice Voting**. Or use the enclosed ballot and return it to us by mail. We must have your vote by **December 31, 2014.**

On the Cover: Tiffany Landscape, *hooked by Jean Ann Kuntz, 2013. For more information on this spectacular rug, turn to page 120.*

Table of Contents

RUGS BASED ON ADAPTATIONS

RUGS BASED ON PRIMITIVE DESIGNS

HONORABLE MENTIONS

Meet the Judges

Each year a new panel of judges takes on the daunting task of evaluating *Celebration* entries. Imagine the enormity of the task: each entry comes with 4 separate photos, so in a field of 200 entries the judges will review and evaluate a total of 800 photographs. With our current system of online judging, the process is more judge-friendly than in the days when judges traveled here to view the entries, one slide at a time. But consider the task that they face: even sitting in their own homes in a favorite chair with a cup of coffee nearby, it is an enormous commitment of time and energy. Hours and hours of concentration, deliberation, and careful consideration; the judges essentially commit one week in early January to *Celebration* judging. All for the love of rug hooking. It is their expertise and wide-ranging experience that makes *Celebration* work so well; they are the foundation of the whole enterprise.

And so we extend our heartfelt thanks to these four judges and to all the judges who have gone before them. And, please . . . if you have an opportunity, be sure to thank a judge. Their contributions cannot be overstated.

Pris Buttler

Pris is an artist with many years' experience as a graphic designer. She has an AA degree in graphic design from Pikes Peak Community College in Colorado Springs, Colorado. Pris has been featured in *Celebration X* and *Celebration XI* and *Rug Hooking* magazine. She designs patterns and has taught on the national curcuit since 1999. She is also represented by Atlanta Art Gallery in Georgia; Stellers Art Gallery in Jacksonville, Florida; and Cohen-Rese Gallery in San Francisco, California. She has sold her folk art through a number of nationally known folk art galleries: The Modern Primitive in Atlanta, Georgia; House of Blues in Myrtle Beach, South Carolina, and Orlando, Florida; America Oh Yes in Hilton Head, South Carolina; and Americarts in Sopporo, Japan. She has earned many awards over the years in both folk art and representational art.

Carrie Martin

To Carrie, rug hooking is the ultimate fiber art. She believes that rug hooking artists have the greatest variety in choice of color, textures, and materials of all textile artists and the subjects are endless. Through rug hooking, an artist's work can express who he or she is:

personal views, likes, and dislikes. Traveling the country to teach is a delight for Carrie—she enjoys meeting fellow artists and encouraging them to find their way. Look for her in Duluth, Minnesota; in Sebring, Florida; at Punderson Rug Camp in Ohio; and in New Orleans. She teaches at many private workshops throughout the country.

Peg Irish

Peg has been rug hooking since 1980. In 1989, she won best-in-show at the League of New Hampshire Craftsmen's annual juried show. Since then, her work

has been selected for more than three dozen juried and invitational exhibits, including a two-woman exhibition at the Cahoon Museum of American Art on Cape Cod and international shows that traveled to Japan. Most recently she was selected to be a featured artist at the Green Mountain Rug Hooking Guild's Hooked in the Mountains. Her work has appeared in two dozen publications, most notably in three volumes of

Fiberarts Design Books and Anne-Marie Littenberg's *Hooked Rug Portraits*. Peg has lectured and taught numerous workshops throughout the Northeast, and she has served as the newsletter editor of The International Guild of Hand-hooking Rugmakers. She is also a juried member of the League of New Hampshire Craftsmen.

Bev Conway

Nationally known teacher, designer, and owner of Beverly Conway Designs, Bev has over 20 years' experience in the world of rug hooking. Her work has been published in many books and magazine articles. She is a past vice president of the Green Mountain Rug Hooking Guild in Vermont, and in 2011 she was celebrated as a featured artist by the Green Mountain Guild at their biannual rug show. She is the originator of the true "Secret Message Technique," which she teaches in workshops around the country.

ORIGINAL DESIGNS

Angel Oak

While on a vacation to Savannah, Georgia, and Charleston, South Carolina, Lyle Drier took a break from photographing the ironwork that she loves to capture this picture of a famed tree on John's Island outside Charleston. "The tree is estimated to be 500 to 1,000 years old, and it spreads over an entire city block," she said. "Many of the huge limbs grow down to the ground in places. It is a wondrous thing to behold."

When sifting through her photographs of the tree, she decided on one that included her sister. "She was photographing the tree at the same time we were," Lyle says. "Having her in the rug provided perspective on the size of the tree and added to the memories of the trip."

Lyle planned the colors based on the photograph—natural colors for the tree and black for the wrought iron—with some alterations, which included neutrals for the sky. She used spot-dyes over new wool for much of the canopy. For the ground, she chose found wool overdyed with onion skin.

The most challenging part of completing this rug was the border. "First, I had to decide which of the many wrought iron examples I had photographed to use," she says. "In many cases I ended up using just parts of wrought iron gates and fences. Then, they needed to be hooked in #2- and 3-cut wool to get the detail. It was time-consuming, but worth it!"

Lyle's favorite part of the finished rug is the tree, especially the trunk and the moss-covered branches. Filling the entire frame with one tree gave Lyle a sense of accomplishment and reminded her daily just how impressive the still-living tree is. She followed the photograph closely, making subtle changes to increase the feeling of depth within the tree branches and the overall immensity of the tree as a whole.

Lyle finished the rug with cording and black wool. The completed rug hangs over the computer desk in her den.

LYLE DRIER
WAUKESHA, WISCONSIN

Lyle saw an article about hooked rugs in an issue of Woman's Day *and started hooking her own rugs in 1971 as accents for the antiques in her home. Since then, she's hooked more than 180 projects. Angel Oak is her ninth rug to be featured in Celebration.*

In the Judges' Words

- *Nice original idea*
- *Love how the artist achieved depth in the tree*
- *Excellent*

8 • *Celebration XXIV 2014*

Angel Oak, 42" x 35", #2- to 6-cut wool on monk's cloth.
Designed and hooked by Lyle Drier, Waukesha, Wisconsin, 2013. DENNIS DRIER

Barn Lust

In all her years of rug hooking, Trish Johnson has never sold one of her rugs. The reason behind that just may be that every rug she hooks has deep personal value built on memories and special interests. Her most recent rug, *Barn Lust*, is a combination of both.

"I chose this design because Simcoe Count Museum wanted hooked rugs of Ontario barns for a show called *Barn Raising*," she says. "I love to hook landscapes that include old buildings, and I like to hook places that are significant to my own family's history. There are no barns in my family's history, but there is this Ontario barn that I hope becomes a part of my family's future."

Trish's daughter, Laura, currently farms the land around this old dairy barn, growing hazelnut trees and heirloom tomatoes in a wide array of colors for her heirloom seed business. Laura hopes to own the property and convert the barn into a house for her family one day.

Trish stuck with the colors in the original photograph when she color planned the rug. She dip dyed the wool for the sky and spot dyed many of the greens. The remainder of the wool, including tweeds for the fields and white angora yarn for the lightest values in the clouds, came from her personal stash.

Trish's favorite part of the rug is the sky, "because it

- *Great mood piece; I can feel summer*
- *Excellent shading on barns*
- *Really like the grasses in the foreground*

Barn Lust, 36¹/₂" x 14", #4-cut wool on linen. Designed and hooked by Trish Johnson, Toronto, Ontario, Canada, 2013.
NORTHERN ARTISTS

works," she says. "It shades down from dark to light at the horizon, and the clouds shade too. There is higher contrast between the clouds and the sky closer to the viewer and lower contrast between the sky and the clouds closer to the horizon. I hope that the viewer is drawn into the image."

Her hooking process was to start with the clouds first. "It was an act of faith that it would all work out when I hooked in the background," she says.

To finish the rug, Trish rolled the edge of the backing to the front and whipped over it with beige wool. The completed rug is currently on display in the Simcoe County Museum's *Barn Raising* exhibition.

TRISH JOHNSON
TORONTO, ONTARIO, CANADA

Trish learned to hook in 1978 from her Aunt Eliza, who encouraged her to pick up a hook and fill in the sky on a project. She started rug hooking for herself in 1988 and has hooked more than 43 rugs to date. Barn Lust marks her eighth rug to appear in Celebration.

Birds and Birdhouses

Long-distance relationships are challenging by nature, but for Karen Maddox and Sondra Kellar, tossing rug hooking into the mix made it just a little easier.

Sondra Kellar is Karen Maddox's daughter. About seven years ago, Sondra decided she wanted to learn to hook, so Karen taught her by long distance. They used email and telephone to close the gap between them.

Karen originally designed the pattern for this rug for a student who wanted to hook birds in a tree with some birdhouses. Both she and the student researched different birdhouses and birds so there would be a variety, and then Karen placed them in various spots in the tree. A bird admirer herself, Karen was familiar with most of the birds, so their color played an important part in choosing which bird would look best in a certain place.

Sondra started hooking the birdhouses, the tree, many of the birds and some of the background dirt, but her available hooking time dwindled as her everyday life picked up speed. So Karen offered to pick up where her daughter left off. Karen hooked a few more birds and the sky, whipped the edges with yarn, and put on the rug tape.

Karen's favorite part of the rug is the stained glass window. "We were trying to make the rug fairly realistic, so most of the colors chosen were found in nature," she says. However, we could expand our vision with the stained glass and used a wonderful spot dye that seemed to make the church windows 'sing.'"

Sondra likes the birds the best and turned to the robins, cardinals, and other birds flying around her backyard as inspiration. She used textures in some of the wings, such as on the cardinal, to get the different colors. She also used a checkerboard style of different colors and textures in a couple of the birds to simulate a mottled look. "I used a #3 cut for the first time," she says. "Hooking them let me practice my fine cut shading."

The mother-daughter labor of love is shared equally between the two women: Sondra displays the rug in her home for six months; then, it's Karen's turn for six months.

In the Judges' Words

- *A bird-lover's delight*
- *Good job balancing the color*
- *Great graphic piece*

Birds and Birdhouses, 48″ x 48″, #3-, 4-, and 5-cut wool on monk's cloth.
Designed by Karen Maddox; hooked by Karen Maddox and Sondra Kellar, Kerrville, Texas, 2013.

KAREN MADDOX AND SONDRA KELLAR
KERRVILLE, TEXAS

Sondra learned to hook from her mother, Karen. Between the two they've hooked 60-plus rugs. Sondra recently followed in her mother's footsteps to become a McGown certified rug hooking teacher. Karen has been hooking rugs for 16 years; Sondra for 7.

Charlotte in the Lupines

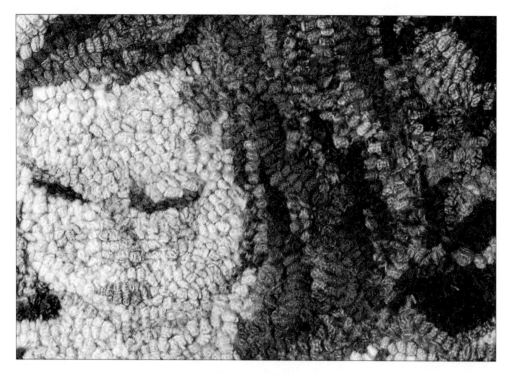

In the Judges' Words

- Very sweet and touching; a delightful portrait
- Excellent use of lights and darks
- Beautiful finishing

Portraits are often about capturing the essence of a figure. While head shots are nice, photographs that capture the interests, personality, and emotions of the subject do a much better job of capturing the viewer's interest.

Stephanie found this to be true when she chose to hook this photograph of her three-year-old granddaughter. "I decided on this project because the photograph captures my granddaughter in a moment of examining nature, which she continues to be intrigued by." The intent downward glance, the careful handling of the flowers, and the background provided by Mother Nature, all come together to highlight this youngster's interests.

This rug was designed and hooked as part of a class with Elizabeth Black. "When I found myself in her class at camp—and without a pet, which is the usual subject of her teaching—I asked if I could tackle this subject instead. I found her face and hands were the most challenging. Finding the right colors that were true to the photograph took time."

While she usually prefers a wider cut, Stephanie stepped out of her comfort zone with this rug. "I found much more detail can be accomplished with fine cut," she says. "Elizabeth Black really made you open your eyes to see what the visual is guiding you to do. I have learned to trust my instincts more by doing this piece."

Stephanie dyed some wool and purchased others. She also used a large assortment of worms, which played a big role in her favorite parts of the completed rug: the sunlight shining off her granddaughter's hair and the lupines that surround her. "I was lucky to have someone in that class who brought a bucket of worms so that I could choose all the colors in Charlotte's hair," she says.

Stephanie finished the rug by overcasting the edges with yarn into the binding tape on the back. The completed rug will be displayed at her son's house in Brookline, Massachusetts, after the *Celebration* exhibition is over. Until then, Stephanie has granted him rug visitation rights when his family comes to see her in Texas.

STEPHANIE STOKES
SAN ANTONIO, TEXAS

Stephanie started to hook rugs in the 1970s after ordering a kit from an advertisement in McCall's magazine. From that hooked rendition of an orange crate advertisement, she went on to complete 17 rugs and has 10 more planned. This is her first rug to be featured in Celebration.

Charlotte in the Lupines, 21¹/₂″ x 16³/₄″, #3- and 4-cut wool on cotton warp. Designed and hooked by Stephanie Stokes, San Antonio, Texas, 2013. MARC BENNETT

Ever So Serene

Diana likes to add her own contemporary and unique view to each subject she portrays while still striving to create realism. "Every piece is an expression of an adventure of my passion to create," she says, "capturing for a moment the shining elusive element of a special time, an endless moment of tranquility, as life around hurries by." With *Ever So Serene*, she has succeeded in translating a beautiful, calming image into wool.

Diana was inspired to pick this subject by both the challenge of recreating nature's beauty and the desire to express herself. In this scene, a duck floats calmly on the surface. The water ripples out around it, perhaps by the constantly moving legs under the surface. While the viewer doesn't see the surrounding landscape, they can piece together an image in their mind's eye based on the colors that are reflected in the undulating surface of the water.

Diana chooses a color palette for each hooked piece, enjoying the richness and comfort of the color combinations she picks. Here she chose a palette of rich green foliage color intermingled with brighter oranges and yellows that suggest the bright blossoms of summer. She used a variety of dip dyes and overdyes as well as mottled and solid pieces of wool. The wool from this piece came from 100% new wool and a recycled deep emerald green wool coat that she used in the deepest shades of green in the ripples.

Ever So Serene, 31" x 16¹/₂", #3-cut wool on linen. Designed and hooked by Diane Ayles, Huntsville, Ontario, Canada, 2012.

In the Judges' Words

- *I like the pointillistic nature of this work*
- *Title describes the piece perfectly*
- *Magnificent*

Diana's favorite part of this rug is the surface of the water. "The color of the summer trees mimic themselves in the ripples of the reflection of the water as the summer sun filters light through them, creating a beautiful reflection of colors and textures," she says.

Her biggest challenge in hooking this piece was "feeling the peace and calm of the presence of the duck and translating that to the viewer," she says. "The transformation of this piece was incredible and I feel I named it well. It is a beautiful reminder of nature's tranquility."

Diana had the piece professionally framed. It currently hangs in a private collection.

DIANA AYLES
HUNTSVILLE, ONTARIO, CANADA

Diana has always had a passion for creating and has been an artist her whole life. She credits her family and friends with her introduction to rug hooking because they inspired her to be true to herself and encouraged her to pursue her creative passions. Ever So Serene is her second rug to be featured in Celebration.

Fab 5

Nancy feels that she had absolutely no choice in whether to hook this rug. "The photo that inspired this rug was taken in June 2011 to celebrate our 20 years of friendship," she says. "As I scrolled through the pictures taken on the beach, this one jumped out and immediately I felt my creative mojo doing a happy dance. I knew it had to be my next rug, and I couldn't wait to get home to get started."

Nancy's color planning for this rug started in Photoshop, where she enhanced the original colors of the photograph, which was taken on a gray, overcast day. Nancy found that by delving into her extensive stash she was able to come up with a combination of recycled, off-the-bolt, and hand-dyed wools without having to make any new purchases.

While the premise of the rug is based on Nancy's deep and lasting friendship with a specific group of friends, she purposely left the faces of the women in the hooked piece blank. "Since we remain anonymous with no faces visible, I think it's easier for others to imagine themselves in that setting with a special group of friends," she says. "Personally, *Fab 5* evokes wonderful, fun memories of not only that weekend, but also a special part of my life."

The symbolism in the rug strikes Nancy as her favorite part of this hooking. "It's fitting that we gals are viewed from behind since it was in our long-ago past that our special bonds were forged as young mothers, trying to find our ways through the challenges and uncertainty of uncharted waters. And yet there we were, reunited two decades later, completely at ease, sitting quietly side by side, enjoying a well-deserved respite, looking straight ahead into the ever-changing, unpredictable tides in life to come."

The most difficult part of this rug to hook was the seaweed in the sand framing the five women. "It was a nightmare," she says. "I fought with it and re-hooked it several times with different colors until I felt it wasn't too distracting."

Nancy rolled and bound the edges. The finished rug hangs on the wall in her new studio.

NANCY ECKLUND QUALLS
OVIEDO, FLORIDA

Nancy saw her first hooked rug in 2006 on The Carol Duvall Show *and immediately ordered a kit from eBay. While the kit wasn't an ideal introduction to rug hooking (strips too thick and hook too fine), her neighbor knew a friend who rug hooked. . . . She has hooked 16 rugs to date. Fab 5 is her first rug to be included in* Celebration.

Fab 5, 30" x 24", #6-cut wool on linen. Designed and hooked by Nancy Ecklund Qualls, Oviedo, Florida, 2012.

In the Judges' Words

- *Excellent skin tones*
- *Love the monochromatic swimwear*
- *Nicely done beach scene*

Facescape in Three Parts

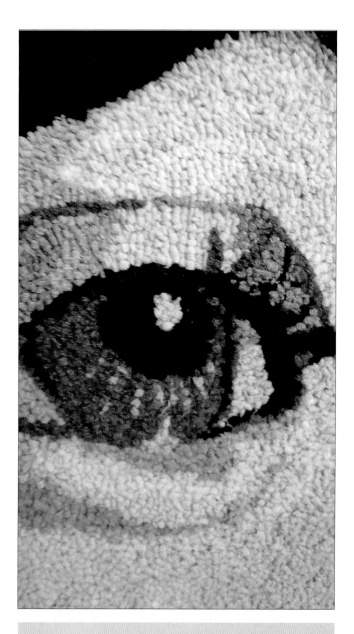

The face in this hooked piece is Carol Koerner's. "One morning, I woke up about half an hour before the alarm clock and an idea popped into my head. Inspirations seem to come to me this way, giving me just enough time to mull over how to accomplish whatever it was before having to start my day. I made a quick thumbnail sketch with notes as soon as I got out of bed. I thought it would be interesting to hook an extreme close-up of a face and treat it as thought it was a rolling landscape with its details of hills, bushes, ponds, crevices and so on," she says.

For this piece, Carol only needed to choose one color. "I mulled over my color choices for a few weeks and had to go with blue," she says. "Landscape grass green did not seem proper for a complexion, and warm colors just didn't please me. So blue-leaning-toward turquoise it was."

Carol dyed every bit of wool, except for the dark navy blue. She prepared one dye bath and left each piece of wool in the dye pot for incremental increases of time to get the different swatches she needed. All of the fabric was recycled from thrift shop skirts.

Carol's favorite part of hooking this rug was its large scale. "I really enjoyed hooking the eyes," she says. "Because the eyes have been enlarged so very much, the attention given to the details and folds surrounding them was much keener. Where I was used to hooking in a single line of loops in a smaller face, I found I had to hook in many more to get the same effect."

Her biggest challenge was something that many rug hookers find challenging in other rugs: large expanses. "In between the eyes, nose, and mouth there is a lot of space, but that space isn't flat. I had to use different shades from dark to light to create the hilly contours."

To finish the rug, Carol hand stitched binding tape and added sleeves for dowels. The finished rug hangs on her dining room wall.

CAROL KOERNER
BETHESDA, MARYLAND

Carol started to hook rugs after her father passed away. An avid rug hooker, he loved giving his hooked rugs to his children and grandchildren. Carol has finished 40 rugs since 1995. Facescape in Three Parts is her 10th rug to be featured in Celebration.

In the Judges' Words

- *Wonderful modeling of the piece*
- *Artist has created a thought-provoking piece*
- *Wow! Beautiful!*

Facescape in Three Parts, 25" x 34", #3-cut wool on linen. Designed and hooked by Carol Koerner, Bethesda, Maryland, 2013.

Ivy's Mona Lisa Smile

Suzanne Gunn was thrilled to find that she'd captured a Mona Lisa–like smile among the photographs she'd taken at a family gathering. "My granddaughter, Ivy, was lying on the deck taking in everything that was going on," she says. "I caught her watching us with that special smile of hers. I wondered what was going through her very imaginative mind. That enigmatic smile of hers always made me think of the *Mona Lisa's* smile."

Suzanne color planned this rug based on the photograph. She used casserole, dip dyeing, and overdyeing techniques over Dorr natural wool and Fleece Artist yarn. The wool for the sand was left over from extra yardage she had dyed for a beach portrait of her grandson, Argus.

Suzanne's favorite part of this rug is her granddaughter's smile. "By cropping just her mouth and then enlarging it, I was able to remove any distractions and I could just focus on the mouth," she says. "Still, it took several attempts for me to be happy with it. It is as close to the real image as I could get but not as close as if I were using oils or water color."

A common challenge in hooking portraits doesn't happen during the hooking process but crops up afterward. "I always tell the person I'm hooking that their hooking will be a close likeness—not exact—so they won't be disappointed, but I always want it to be an exact likeness. A strip of wool has its limitations!" she says. "Every portrait I do gets me closer to this goal. This is the challenge for me in every portrait and what keeps me in love with this medium."

The most challenging part of the piece was deciding on the best background. "I did not want to hook Ivy on the cottage deck," she says. "So after much deliberation I decided to put her on a neutral background. I did not want any visual distractions from the figure."

Suzanne placed the rug in a metal frame. It hangs in her husband's office beside a hooked New Zealand beach scene of their grandson, Argus.

SUZANNE GUNN
NOVA SCOTIA, CANADA

Suzanne taught herself to hook in 1978 after admiring a very old inch rug at a friend's house. She designed her first rug in 2004 and has hooked 77 rugs to date. Ivy's Mona Lisa Smile is her sixth rug to be included in the pages of Celebration.

Ivy's Mona Lisa Smile, 35" x 28", wool strips and fleece on linen. Designed and hooked by Suzanne Gunn, Nova Scotia, Canada, 2013.

In the Judges' Words

- *This absolutely screams summer*
- *Contour hooking in the sand gives me the feeling of being there*
- *Beautifully restrained piece*

Lessons from Our Son

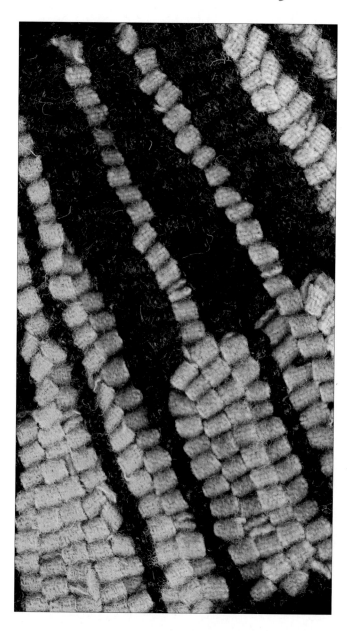

P at Shafer began this hooked rug as a tribute to her oldest son, Tim. "As I started to work on it, thinking of all the lessons that we teach our children, I realized that it was the lessons that they teach us that are sometimes overlooked but so important," she says.

The piano keys and music score represent Tim's love of music and his fabulous singing voice. The artist's brush symbolizes an amazing talent that allowed him to establish a solid career as an art director and graphic artist. The star, top hat, and theater masks reflect his love of theater, both on stage and behind the scenes. But it is the crayons—his "weapons of choice from childhood"—that tell of the lessons that their son taught Pat and her husband.

"Always dream big."

"Laugh, dance, and sing . . . often and loudly."

"Listen to your imagination . . . it will lead you to wonderfully unexpected surprises."

"And above all, believe in magic, because it's all magic."

Pat's son passed away 11 years ago, but Pat has found that the lessons that she spelled out in this rug lead her through life every day.

Pat color planned the rug with the help of Pris Buttler. She had originally pictured the rug in black and white, "but Pris took one look at it and said, 'How about the color wheel?' At that precise moment I was off and hooking. It was so right! It was such fun transitioning those colors into the lessons and the remainder of the rug. It was like dancing through a rainbow."

Pat needed only three months to hook the rug. She used new and recycled wool that had been primarily overdyed and some spot dyes. "Hooking this rug was like taking a journey, and I really milked it at the end," she says. "It was one of those rugs that you travel through and don't want to be over."

To finish the rug, Pat whipped the edges with yarn. The completed rug hangs in the family room of her home.

PAT SHAFER
OMAHA, NEBRASKA

Pat started in fiber arts with quilting and punch needle but became fascinated with the ability to paint with wool through hooked rugs about nine years ago. She has hooked more than 50 rugs and pillows since then. Lessons from Our Son is her first rug to be featured in Celebration.

In the Judges' Words

- *Good use of color and dull grays*
- *Your keyboard dances!*
- *Lovely letters*

Lessons from Our Son, 32" x 24", #4, 6-, and 8-cut wool on linen. Designed and hooked by Pat Shafer, Omaha, Nebraska, 2013. SCOTT AVERY

Looking Down from Delphi

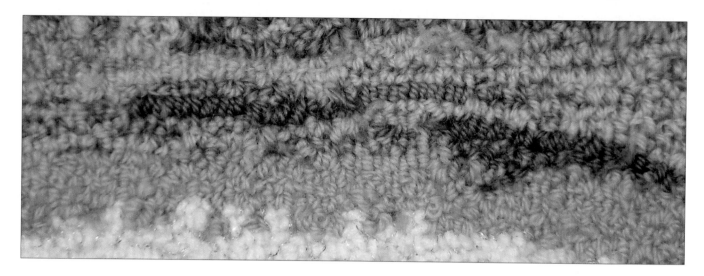

Arlette Spencer has a number of hooked pieces to her name, but she has yet to hook a rug. "Rugs seem like an enormous undertaking and I can't bear the thought of walking on all that work," she says. "I have hooked pillows of various sizes, a tote bag front, a small framed piece, and a small wall hanging. I like the varying details of these smaller pieces."

While Arlette's rug, *Looking Down from Delphi*, is not overly small, she still does not consider it a rug because of the framing and its placement on the wall in her dining room.

Arlette chose this landscape from a number of photographs taken during a recent trip to Greece. To match the colors as closely as possible to the original photograph, she dyed the wool strips used at the bottom of the hooking using the open pan method. The remainder of the hooking material came from a variety of commercial yarns. She hooked the background in 4-strand tapestry yarn and the village in a very white, shimmery yarn laced with silver thread.

Arlette's favorite part of this rug is its design because it reminds her so vividly of her trip to Greece. "We were at the site where the Oracle of Delphi made her prophecies," she says. "We found out that at the place where the Oracle sat there were hallucinatory gases coming up, which contributed to her visions. This picture upon which the hooking was based was taken from the hotel balcony in Delphi."

She found the most difficult part of hooking this rug to be separating and combining the four strands of tapestry wool in various combinations to achieve the colors she wanted. The most effective way to make a decision was also very time-consuming: "I just had to try each one out to see if it was right and be persistent," she says.

To frame the rug, Arlette stretched the hooked rug over ½-inch foam core and fastened it in place with stickpins. She then took the stretched piece to a framer who graciously conceded to her request to mat and frame the piece without glass.

ARLETTE SPENCER
MEDICINE HAT, ALBERTA, CANADA

Arlette was on a trip to the Maritimes in 2009 when she discovered rug hooking—the perfect handwork for her new retired status! After an hour-long introduction at the Highland Heart Hookery, she was ready to start. She has hooked an untotaled number of pieces since then. This is her first rug to be chosen for Celebration.

In the Judges' Words

- *The depth achieved gets my applause*
- *Love the combination of yarns and fabric*
- *Very nicely done*

Looking Down from Delphi, 21⅞" x 15½", #4- and 6-cut wool, assorted yarns, and silver thread on monk's cloth. Designed and hooked by Arlette Spencer, Medicine Hat, Alberta, Canada, 2013.

Low Tide at Blue Rocks

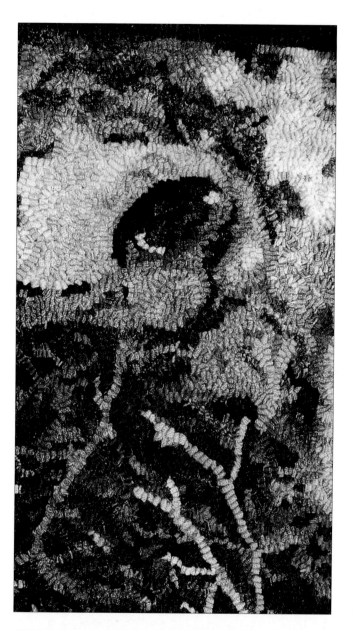

As a retired biology teacher, Betty Calvert found it quite natural to drift toward a portrait of a tidal pool when she planned her most recent hooked rug. The abundance of organisms in a tidal pool also fell right into her modus operandi for her current rug projects. "Right now I am enjoying painting with wool," she says. "I like using a large variety of colors and textures."

Betty began color planning for the rug with the help of Diane Stoffel during a class at Ragg Time and then continued to fill out the color plan on her own. She used spot dyes, casserole dyes, dip dyes, and parts of swatches to create the vast number of colors and shades she needed for this piece. She combed through both new and recycled wools with an eye toward whatever wool would give her the look she was seeking.

When asked to pick a favorite part of her rug, Betty has difficulty. "I cannot choose one favorite part because I like each area that my eye falls on," she says. "When I am working on a rug like this that I am passionate about, I am thrilled when each element comes alive." Rather than choose one area, Betty notes that she likes the depth she was able to achieve in the piece through careful design and placement of the various elements.

Choosing the colors for the different seaweeds was the most challenging part of hooking this rug. "I researched the seaweeds that grow along the Atlantic coast," she says, "then I searched through my wool stash or dyed colors I needed." Betty hooked some of the seaweed motifs into the border of the blue/green spot dye to give it some additional perspective and to show the often unruly nature of a tide pool. "I did not want my rug to have a definite border, but rather to seem to flow beyond the rug."

Betty finished the rug by whipping the edges with yarn dyed to match the border. The completed rug hangs on her living room wall.

BETTY CALVERT
ST. CATHARINES, ONTARIO, CANADA

Betty grew up in the Maritimes surrounded by family members who hooked rugs. Her mother taught her the art about 15 years ago, and she has hooked 50 pieces since then. Low Tide at Blue Rocks *is her second rug to be featured in* Celebration.

In the Judges' Words

- *Amazing portrayal of a tidal pool*
- *Rich with color, texture, and recognizable elements*
- *Very cool!*

Low Tide at Blue Rocks, 37" x 23", #3- and 4-cut wool on linen. Designed and hooked by Betty Calvert, St. Catharines, Ontario, Canada, 2013.

Mary Magdalene

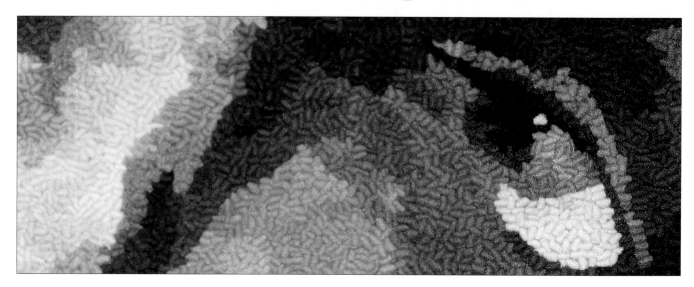

Instead of taking her work home with her, April DeConick takes her art to work. "I am a professor in the Religious Studies Department of Rice University," she says. "When I became chair of the department this year, I wanted to have in my office the presence of a woman that I could look up to for inspiration. So I created *Mary Magdalene*, the one whom Jesus calls in the *Dialogue of the Savior* 'the woman who knows all,' and now she prominently hangs above my desk."

April dyes all the wool she uses in her hooked rugs. In order to achieve the artistic effects she wants in her hooked portraits, she created a dyeing technique that she calls Palette Dyeing. "From three unique dye formulas, I have made 67 colors, each in 8 values," she says. "Just like a painter who has access to unlimited color by mixing paints from a few tubes, I have a complete palette of wool colors and values on hand." For her portrait of Mary Magdalene, she made 15 separate colors, each in 8 values; that translates to 120 different wools. Most were dyed on white, but she did overdye some textures.

The most challenging part of this rug was its size. "The elements like the eyes and mouth were so large that it was

difficult for me to see what I was doing," she says. "I had to lay the rug out on the floor and stand away from it in order to see what I had hooked and whether or not it worked. Mostly it didn't the first time, so that meant that I did a large amount of reverse hooking."

As a new technique to try, April worked to incorporate false colors into the rug, particularly in the shadows. "I wanted to play with greens and see what effect they might have," she says. "What I learned is that green is difficult to use. A little goes a long way. But it is well worth the effort because it brightens shadow areas in ways that cooler colors like blue and purple do not."

To finish the rug, April stretched and stapled it to a 30" by 40" gallery wrapped canvas and had it professionally mounted in an oversized black frame. "When people see it for the first time, they are sure it is an oil painting," she says.

In the Judges' Words

- *Subject is interesting from afar and up close*
- *A very painterly approach*
- *Bravo!*

APRIL DeCONICK
HOUSTON, TEXAS

April's first rug was hooked as part of a rug hooking class at Waterloo Historical Farm in Michigan in 1995. She's lost count of the exact number of rugs she's hooked over the years, but estimates it's well over 40. This is her third rug to be shown in Celebration.

Mary Magdalene, 40″ x 30″, #6-cut hand-dyed new wool on linen.
Designed and hooked by April DeConick, Houston, Texas, 2013.

Blue Mermaiden

Rug hooking is Donna Hrkman's life. It is her means of personal expression, her way of exploring color and design, and a vehicle for sharing thoughts and feelings about a variety of topics. One way to accomplish this is to take part in designers' challenges. In this challenge, each rug hooker was tasked with creating a rug that would be an exploration of color, mood, and emotion. Donna was asked to choose a color, design a rug that exemplified how she felt about that color, and write a brief description about the project. The result was *Blue Mermaiden*.

Donna designed the color for this rug around her theme. "Because the purpose of this rug was to express a mood through a particular color, it was important to use primarily a monochromatic palette," she says. "The key then is to have enough contrast to prevent the rug from blending into visual mush. By including a variety of lights and darks in high contrast and adding a few elements of a complementary color, the character of the rug is clear."

"I started with a monochromatic color palette with a range of blues from an icy white to a deep navy blue," she says. "I introduced the complement of orange into the composition for contrast and movement." Donna used Dorr white wool for the bulk of the rug but hooked in some thick, textured wool yarn for variety.

Donna especially likes the serene expression of the mermaiden, but loves the sense of fun and frolic that the sea horses bring to the scene. "I found a unique way to portray a fantasy image, a nontraditional portrayal of a mermaid. Only her tail fin identifies her as a mermaid, and the color and pattern of the water above and around her reinforces that image."

To finish the rug, Donna wrapped cotton cording under the edge of the linen backing and whipped it with navy blue yarn. The rug travels with her to teaching engagements across the country and is currently rolled up in her studio awaiting the next trip.

DONNA HRKMAN
DAYTON, OHIO

Donna held out as long as she could under pressure from her friends to try rug hooking, and once she did, she "totally fell in love." She's hooked close to 100 rugs in the past 10 years and donates or sells most of what she creates. Blue Mermaiden is her seventh rug to be featured in Celebration.

Blue Mermaiden, 26" x 18", #3-cut hand-dyed wool on bleached linen. Designed and hooked by Donna Hrkman, Dayton, Ohio, 2013. DANIEL HRKMAN

In the Judges' Words

- *Very interesting concept and use of complements*
- *She's beautiful!*
- *Good job portraying sea horse above and below the tail*

Night Life in the Country

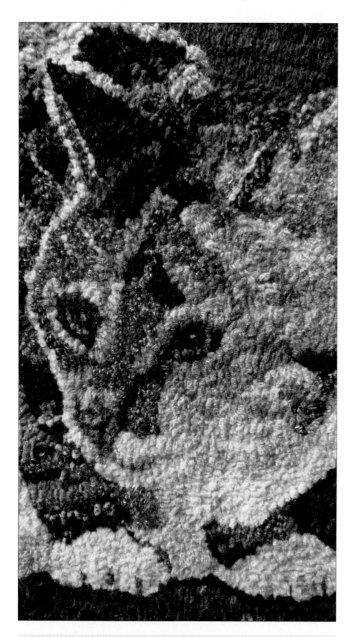

Juliana signed up for a class with Jon Ciemiewicz and decided to create a rug of her cat, Hope, in a natural setting. The inspiration for the design came from a gardening catalogue, a watercolor painting, and a children's book that she loved to read to her kids when they were younger.

Juliana planned the color scheme around her cat. She chose the purple decorative cabbages instead of the traditional green ones because she thought the colors would work better with the shadows of the night scene. For the cat, she used as-is and over dyed textures. For the cabbages, she dyed multiple value swatches and a spot dye. She created the colors for the moon in a casserole dye. The sky was hooked from her mother's gray pantsuit that she overdyed in a combination of pan dyes.

While the cat is Juliana's favorite part of the rug—specifically, the cat's nose—Juliana also found the cat to be the most difficult part of the rug to hook. "The picture I had was a mirror image of the cat in the rug," she says. "After a weekend of frustration, I was able to flip the image on my computer." Getting the strips and coloration on the cat right was important to show the cat's muscles and bunched posture as it lay in wait.

Juliana brought depth to the composition with the repeating shapes of the cabbages and the cat. The horizontal hooking of the sky contrasts with the squiggly lines of the ground and intersects at an angle with the line of the cabbages, deepening the plane. The mouse, which is not obvious at first glance, comes to the forefront as the viewer traces the line of sight from the cat's eyes.

Juliana rolled and whipped the edges with alpaca yarn that she had dyed to match the background. The finished rug hangs in her family room.

JULIANA KAPUSTA
TELFORD, PENNSYLVANIA

Textiles were always Juliana's craft of choice, but rug hooking took over the top spot when she saw it demonstrated at a living history fair in 1998. Since then she's hooked nine rugs plus a few small mats. Night Life in the Country is her second hooked piece to be featured in Celebration.

In the Judges' Words

- *Calico cat is outstanding*
- *Made me want to know more about the artist's thoughts in creating the design*
- *Incredible use of complements and triangulation*

Night Life in the Country, 36" x 25", #4-and 5-cut wool on rug warp, Juliana Kapusta, Telford, Pennsylvania, 2013.

Parabolas

Claire Molson finds herself inspired by the smallest things. In this case, she turned to a parabola, a geometric term that refers to a U-shaped symmetrical curve in a plane. "I love color and use it freely," she says. "The flow of the parabola simply evolved."

Claire planned the colors based on her own preferences. "I like colors to interact and to clash," she says. Judith Dallegret dyed new wool for Claire's project using spot dyes and abrashed dyes.

The most difficult part of completing this rug was working with the design itself. Claire had to be diligent about keeping the pattern visible in the small rectangles and not placing the same color beside itself. When she finished, she was thrilled with the result. "The 'sides' seem to roll down into the 'floor' of the design," she says. "There's so much movement plus so much color."

The blue diamonds, while they change in tone and intensity, remain a constant throughout the rug. They anchor the undulating design between two opposite corners. The symmetry of the colors as they fill variously compressed and expanded diamonds adds to the optical illusion.

Claire finds that she gained a better understanding of color and shape after she finished this rug. "I learned to never be afraid to try something different," she says. "Go outside the box." Overall, Claire has discovered how much she enjoys expressing her thoughts in color. Each of her rugs has a story, and she hopes to compile the rugs and their stories into a book one day that will likewise inspire and entertain sick children.

Claire's husband David framed the rug, and the completed piece hangs in her bedroom.

Parabolas, 34" x 34" (framed), #6- and 8-cut (with some #4-cut) wool on linen. Designed and hooked by Claire V. Molson, Beaconsfield, Quebec, Canada, 2012. DINO PACIFICI

CLAIRE V. MOLSON
BEACONSFIELD, QUEBEC, CANADA

Sisterly love sometimes extends to hand-work choices, as it did in Claire's case. Claire set aside painting after her sister, Susan, invited her to a rug hooking class and showed her how to paint with wool. She has completed more than 25 rugs in the past 8 years. Parabolas is her first rug to be featured in Celebration.

In the Judges' Words

- Great optical illusion
- Good color choices on a difficult project
- The geometric has so much depth; great job

Redbreast Sunfish

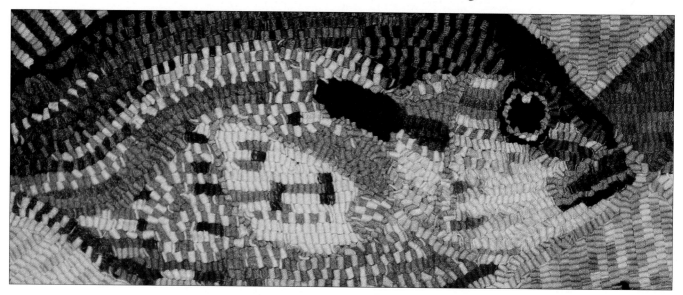

Catherine McGeehin Heilferty's rug began as a birthday present for her husband, John. "I wanted to make him a rug," she says. "I was pretty sure he'd like a fish, but I wanted his favorite. Even though sunfish are usually the littlest in the pond and don't win prizes, he loved their bright colors and feisty nature."

Catherine started her color planning by seeking John's opinions on color. "Somehow, I kept overruling him," she says. "He helped with the bright parts of the fish itself, but the beading and background coloring were my invention. I think we struggled with my desire to keep things abstract and his insistence that it look something like a real fish."

Catherine opted not to do her usual casserole dyeing for the background of this rug. "I tend to overstir everything impatiently," she says. "This project forced me to be careful and patient, a very good exercise." She dyed the background on white wool in light to medium to darker greens with dip dyeing. The remainder of the colors came from recycled wool.

For the background, Catherine employed a technique she noticed in the National Museum of Women in the Arts in Washington, DC. "I had never hooked a background with so much similarity, yet at the same time I wanted to show movement and some change within the scene. A painting on exhibit there included a technique that split the piece into small subsections, almost as if it were cut into pieces and put back together a little off-kilter," she says. "When I decided I wanted motion to hold up the stock-still fish, I thought this technique might work."

Catherine purposely chose a lighter dyed background. "I asked myself a hundred times, 'How can I have so much green in the background, so much green in the fish, and still have everything work together?' The lighter background definitely helped solve part of that problem."

Catherine whipped the edges with yarn to finish the rug. The completed piece hangs in her living room.

CATHERINE
McGEEHIN HEILFERTY
YARDLEY, PENNSYLVANIA

A visit to the Elizabeth LeFort Museum (now the Museum of the Hooked Rug and Home Life) in Cheticamp, Nova Scotia, prompted Catherine to search for more information and opportunities to hook rugs. She's hooked 31 rugs since 2004, and Redbreast Sunfish is her first rug to be featured in Celebration.

In the Judges' Words

- *Beading works so well in the body of the fish*
- *Great background use with geometric shapes*
- *Incredible fish and orange surround*

Redbreast Sunfish, 40" x 29½", #8-cut hand-dyed and recycled wool on linen. Designed and hooked by Catherine McGeehin Heilferty, Yardley, Pennsylvania, 2013.

Rescue of LaBella Julia

Grace Collette chose to hook this scene as a tribute to the US Coast Guard. "My son was fishing off the coast of Maine when a fierce storm swept in," she says. "A rogue wave rolled his vessel and activated the electronic beacon at the bottom of the craft. The signal was picked up by the Coast Guard, which dispatched a jet to lock in the position of the signal while a helicopter came to rescue the men. As the men bobbed in the ocean in survival suits, a brave Coast Guardsman dropped into the waves, swam to the men, and one at a time, got them raised into the buffeting helicopter."

Grace knew that she had to find a way to successfully express the joint anger of the sky and the sea. "A storm would be dark and gloomy," she says, "but my rug couldn't be. I met the problem of boring, dead grays with overdyes. I sat by the ocean under many different weather conditions and tried to analyze the seas and the clouds, especially the values and the shapes. I found there is no 'right way' to hook them as they are different every time you look."

Another challenge was the accuracy of her depiction when it came to the Coast Guard helicopter. "I researched the copters and found their fluorescent chroma seriously clashed with my palette," she says. "After many attempts with actual helicopter color schemes, I decided to stay with the orange color family because it was a great complement to the blue water but use a much softer rusty dip dye. This formed a strong focal point and eliminated the problem of a split focal point."

Grace added lines in the sky to suggest sleet. "They lead the eye from the boat to the helicopter and offset the many curved lines. The jumping dolphin adds a hopeful element. And the seagulls complete a circular composition." Grace included novelty yarns to enhance the splashes of the waves. She cut the large waves in the front in a Waldoboro style for an enhanced perspective.

The finished rug is on display in the Portsmouth Library but will eventually be a gift for her son.

In the Judges' Words

- *Angry sea created by use of so many textures, values, and different fibers*
- *Great waves*
- *What a story*

GRACE E. COLLETTE
RAYMOND, NEW HAMPSHIRE

Grace learned to hook rugs 45 years ago at a YWCA class and then took a 35-year hiatus. Now she is "happily retired and hooking up a storm." Over the 10 years that she's been hooking rugs, she has completed eight rugs. Rescue of LaBella Julia is her fourth rug to be featured in Celebration.

Rescue of La Bella Julia, 30" x 23½", #3-cut wool on linen. Designed and hooked by Grace E. Collette, Raymond, New Hampshire, 2013.

Stanley at Sauble Beach

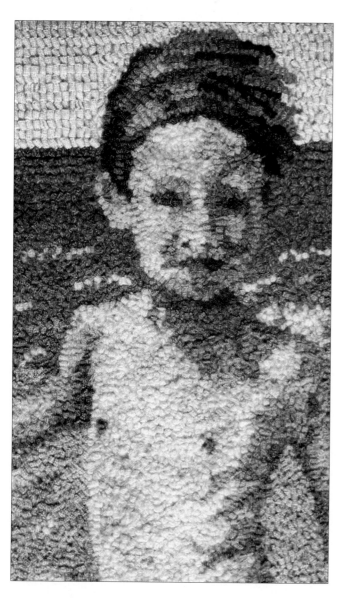

Fumiyo Heinig had been hooking with wide cuts for more than seven years when she decided it was time for a change. "Going through my photo album, I came across a photo I took of my grandson two years ago," she says. "I knew it would be difficult in wide cut as I had to tackle the face and capture a five-year-old's body. So I decided that I'd try the face and hair first in fine cut, and if I could not do it, I'd abort the project."

Using the photograph as a guide, Fumiyo dyed the wool for this project. For the skin and hair, she dyed wool in four small pots with varying values. For the water, sand, and mud, she used a casserole spot dye. For the sky, she created a dip dye.

"I devised a simple method without using dye powder for the bathing suit," she says. "I tore a piece of medium red wool into four pieces. I simmered two of the strips in hot water with Tide. When they became visibly lighter, I pulled one out and dumped it in clear hot water with a little citric acid. When the other became nearly white/pink, I did the same with it. I saved the red liquid, then I put one strip of the original red wool in, adding citric acid until the water cleared." When all was said and done, Fumiyo had the original value of medium red wool and three others to hook the swim trunks.

Fumiyo's favorite part of the hooked rug is the water. "While we were vacationing in Cuba last February, I watched the waves breaking on the sandy beach for hours," she says. Returning home, I redrew small waves and hooked the area quickly while the movement of the sea was fresh in my mind. There are things one cannot get from photographs alone."

Fumiyo placed the rug on plywood with a thin layer of polyester fill in between. She laced the two sides tight to stretch the rug, then she took it to a framer to have the rug professionally framed. The completed rug was given as a gift to Stanley's parents and hangs in their bedroom.

FUMIYO HEINIG
BURLINGTON, ONTARIO, CANADA

Fumiyo kept the idea of starting a hobby on the back burner until she retired. A beginner's class in rug hooking made her decide to work with wool, even though her original intention was to pursue painting. She has hooked eight large rugs and wall hangings and a handful of smaller pieces. This is her second rug to be featured in Celebration.

In the Judges' Words

- *Captures that moment of childhood innocence at the beach*
- *I can feel the sand sticking to my feet*
- *Design is good*

Stanley at Sauble Beach, 21³/₄″ x 28¹/₄″, #3-cut hand-dyed wool on rug warp.
Designed and hooked by Fumiyo Heinig, Burlington, Ontario, Canada, 2013. CHRIS HAYHURST

Tangled

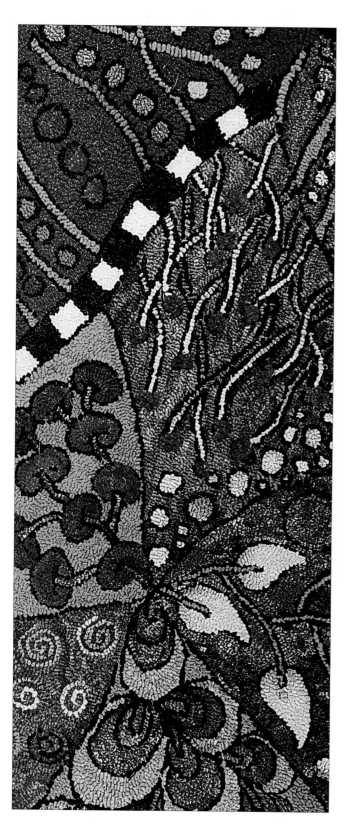

Elissa Thomas Crouch started with the idea of hooking a colorful, cube footstool. As she was working, the piece "just looked flat," she says, "so it became a wall hanging. Then the impact of the design could be seen."

Her inspiration for the design came from attending a class about Zentangle, a drawing method where structured patterns are used to create images. "As I was doing the doodles, I was translating it into my rug hooking—the size of cut to use for outline and how it would impact the size of the design," she says.

Elissa started working on the pattern for this rug by doing a major design element in each square. As she hooked that element, she added more tangles to complement the original element. "I found that the more, the better, as long as I was able to outline it and fill it in."

Elissa color planned the rug based on the Primary Fusion colors that were left over from other projects she had dyed. She used dip, spot, and swatch dyeing to create the colors over 100% Dorr natural wool. "I chose the colors as I went into each design area, making sure it was pleasing to me," she says. "I did this design for me, so it was easy to color plan!"

In order for all those colors and elements to work together, Elissa had to find a way to keep them from blending together as the viewer looked at the artwork. "My favorite part of the rug is the total concept of the design," she says. "All elements had to be outlined to have the animation the design needed. Leaving them out made the design mushy. I outlined each element in order for it to shout out 'Look at me! Color!'"

Elissa finished the edges of the rug with wool strips to match the background. The rug is currently on view at the Joie de Vivre Gallery.

In the Judges' Words

- *Great flow and balance in design and color*
- *From the color chosen to the detail of outlining, this piece is outstanding*

ELISSA THOMAS CROUCH
CAMBRIDGE, MARYLAND

Elissa's friend, Martha Henkle, a member of a McGown guild, introduced her to rug hooking 30 years ago. Elissa doesn't keep track of how many rugs she's hooked as she finds the most pleasure in giving her work away with a hug and a smile. Tangled is her first rug to be featured in Celebration.

Tangled, 47" x 47", #4-cut 100% wool flannel on linen. Designed and hooked by Elissa T. Crouch, Cambridge, Maryland, 2013. DAVE HARP

Tennescott Four Dog Rug— Bernese Mountain Dogs

Barbie Beck-Wilczek started this rug as a loving tribute to four of her best friends, her dogs. But as she hooked, this rug took on even greater meaning. What started out as a joyful project became a challenge and then returned to a source of happy memories.

"I had to be in the right frame of mind and be able to concentrate on the details of each dog so I could capture their personalities to my satisfaction," she says. "Often, I just could not get anything accomplished because I was tired, did not have adequate light, or was not in the right mood to concentrate. I lost the dog on the right soon after I had finished hooking him, and then I lost the dog on the left just as I was finishing the rug. When I was sad, I could not work on the rug."

Barbie color planned the rug based on a favorite photograph of her four Bernese mountain dogs. She purchased dyed wool from several sources and made sure to have a variety of dyeing techniques represented— including spots, dips, and casseroles. Each wool was chosen for its color, shading, and quality. "All the dogs were hooked in a #3-cut wool," she said, "so good quality wool was imperative." In addition to the new wool, she used a small amount of gray recycled wool.

Barbie chose the eyes of the dogs as her favorite part of this rug. "The eyes capture their essence and personalities for me," she says.

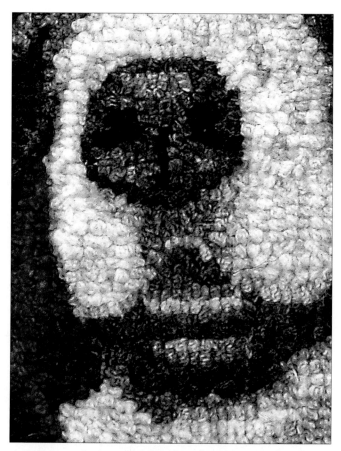

Barbie worked on the rug as she was able off and on for two years. To finish the rug, she whipped the edges with yarn that had been dyed along with the background wool. She sewed a sleeve on the top and one on the bottom of the back to hold stainless steel rods. The completed rug hangs on the wall of her family room where the sunlight will not affect its colors.

BARBIE BECK-WILCZEK
LITTLETON, NEW HAMPSHIRE

Barbie started rug hooking with Gail Dufresne. Her first mat 12 years ago was the Sunflower Inch Mat. *Since then she has hooked about 10 rugs.* Tennescott Four Dog Rug *is her first rug to be featured in* Celebration.

In the Judges' Words

- *Each dog has personality*
- *Darker shades of the throat really create the depth needed to make the dogs come alive*
- *Gorgeous faces*

Tennescott Four Dog Rug—Bernese Mountain Dogs, 45" x 29", #3- and 4-cut wool on rug warp. Designed and hooked by Barbie Beck-Wilczek, Littleton, New Hampshire, 2013.

The Gathering

Rachelle LeBlanc has a degree in fashion design and technique and is a self-taught contemporary rug hooking artist. She put all her skills to work in designing this three-dimensional piece.

The free standing sculpture has no visible seams or seam allowances. A flattened bottom and its overall shape allow the artwork to stand on its own—no supports are needed. Even though the viewer can't see the seam allowances, they are an integral part of the design. "Working on this piece showed me that the rug hooking technique lends itself to any shape and form and has limitless possibilities," she said.

The image of the girl and the birds continues around the back of the piece and on to the bottom. The front of the sculpture tells the story of a girl relaxing and enjoying nature, while the back of the piece shows two birds absconding with the girl's scarf. Perhaps nature is enjoying her presence just as much. The bottom of the piece is also hooked and continues the girl's figure to the underside of the sculpture.

Rachelle color planned this rug using a muted palette with many rich earth tones. The girl's lips, the blueberries, and the green leaves provide pings of color against a neutral color scheme. The bird's wing to the left and a bit of the scarf tempt the viewer to circle the sculpture to see the back side. There the brighter color of the scarf dominates as the birds come out to play.

Rachelle hand dyed all of the wool in a dye pot. She used cashmere and wool.

Her favorite part of this piece is its freedom from any visible seams, making the idea of free standing hooked art even more mysterious. The most difficult part of this rug was working with those hidden seam allowances, which actually are present even if they're invisible. "The seam allowances created some very thick sections," she says, "and at some times, my fingers were blue due to the hook hitting the tips of my fingers over and over in the same place."

Rachelle finished her hooked rug sculpture with Gallery Finish, 100% wool tape, and thread. The completed piece is on display at the Alberta Craft Council.

In the Judges' Words

- *Excellent rendering of texture in clothing and hair*
- *Delightful*
- *A beautiful rendering with a dreamy quality*

RACHELLE LEBLANC
ST. ALBERT, ALBERTA, CANADA

From museum visits in Vermont and Quebec and then research that led her to a 1960s book about rug hooking, Rachelle decided that rug hooking was another way to express her creative energy. Since 2003, she has hooked more than 70 rugs. The Gathering is her second rug to be included in Celebration.

The Gathering, 21" x 20" x 10", #2- to 8-cut wool and cashmere on linen. Designed and hooked by Rachelle LeBlanc, St. Albert, Alberta, Canada, 2013.

Dear Celebration Reader:

Which rugs are your favorites?

The judges have chosen the finalists—now it is up to you to tell us which of these rugs deserve the honor of being named Readers' Choice winners.

Review each of the winning rugs carefully and make your selections. Mark your choices on the attached ballot and be sure to postmark it before December 31, 2014.

Or vote online. Go to *www.rughookingmagazine.com* and look for the *Celebration* Readers' Choice link.

RHM appreciates the time you take to send in your Readers' Choice vote. Please help us honor the rug hooking artists represented within the pages of **Celebration XXIV** by voting for your choice of the best of the best.

Debra Smith

Editor

Toast and Honey

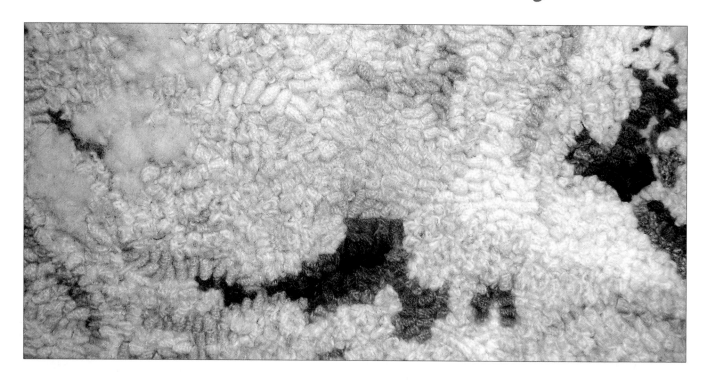

When Susan LaCount had to choose a portrait to hook, she opted not for the human variety but the canine kind. "I am very attached to my dogs [Susan owns five of them], and I had some good photos," she says. "So I wanted to do a portrait of them and not a person." The rug she designed features two of Susan's dogs: Toast, the white dog, and Honey, the gold dog. Toast is Honey's mother.

Susan started this rug as part of a portrait class with Laura Pierce. Susan planned the colors based on the photo she took of the dogs. Susan used all new wool for this project, and she pulled the majority of the wool from her stash of odds and ends and rounded out her selections by buying some small strips. She focused on picking wool that had been casserole dyed or dip dyed. She also used a handful of fuzzy white yarn and some raw roving on Toast.

When Susan compares the finished rug to the photograph, she is very pleased with the overall look of the rug. "I am amazed at how much it looks like the photo," she says. In addition to hooking only curved lines in the dogs' faces, Susan used two other techniques she learned from Laura. The first was to work roving in between the hooked strips in key areas, as seen on the top of Toast's head. The second was the "wide strip rip and wrinkle," seen

above Honey's eye. The addition of these techniques helped Susan to achieve a more varied look.

Susan found it difficult to determine which strip of material would give the effect of shadow and curl in the dogs' hair. She finally decided to put less thought into the process and just pull strips from piles that had been sorted into shades. "I learned that I was intimidated by the idea of all the shades and didn't think I would be able to make it look right," she says. "But it was easier than I thought."

Susan whipped the edge with a rough yarn and stitched a strip to the back that would house a dowel. The rug hangs against a sage green wall in her living room.

SUSAN LaCOUNT
ROCKY MOUNTAIN HOUSE, ALBERTA, CANADA

Susan was introduced to rug hooking in 2003 by her sister-in-law and finds that it's the perfect handwork to keep her busy while she's watching TV or relaxing. She estimates that she's hooked between 30 and 40 rugs in the past 11 years. This is her first rug to be featured in Celebration.

Toast and Honey, 19½" x 16", mostly #7-cut wool, Susan LaCount, Rocky Mountain House, Alberta, Canada, 2013.

In the Judges' Words

- Nice design concepts going on throughout
- I know the artist loves these two
- Beautiful perspective

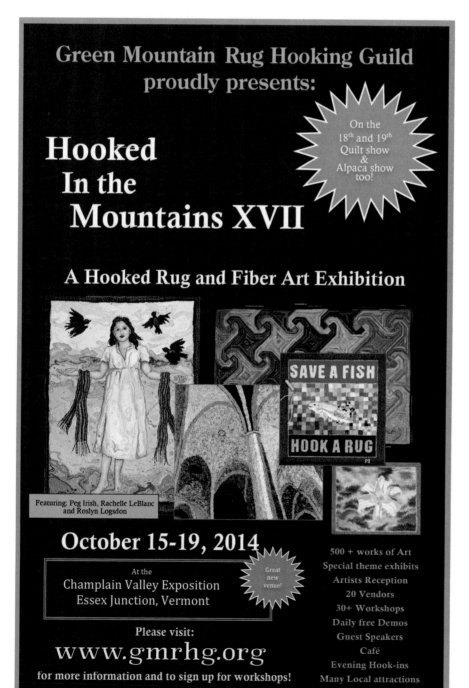

Birches

Beth Morris saw a classmate at the Rock River Ruggers camp working this design and knew instantly that she wanted to hook the same pattern. "I wanted to combine the realism and starkness of the birch tree trunks with the highly impressionistic and colorful fall foliage," she says.

Carol Kassera, who designed the rug, dyed all the wool swatches for the tree trunks over new wool. Carol also spot dyed new wool in autumn colors for the foliage; Beth supplemented the fall colors with wool pieces from her own stash.

Beth enjoys the interplay of the various foliage colors and the way the colors move from the richer and deeper range in the lower half of the piece to lightness and brightness as the viewer's eye travels up the tree trunks. The heavy reds and oranges change to soft yellows and greens that finally end at the blue sky. "I learned that a carefully practiced technique, as demonstrated in the hooked tree trunks, when combined with the free-form hooking of the foliage, can produce a wonderful result."

The trees took a lot of effort and concentration. "Hooking those tree trunks so that they looked dimensional and like real birch wood was my greatest challenge," she says. "Because I started the piece at a multiday rug camp, I was able to perfect the birch trunk technique under the watchful eye of my teacher." Beth credits Carol as being instrumental in teaching her how to hook the trunks in a "bowed horizontal" manner to simulate the dimensional roundness of the trunks.

BETH MORRIS
NAPERVILLE, ILLINOIS

Beth learned rug hooking in 1990 in order to hook a rug for the front hallway in her home. Since then she's hooked 60 pieces, including everything from wall hangings to dolls. Birches is her first rug to be featured in Celebration.

Birches, 18" x 24", #3- and 4-cut wool on linen.
Designed by Carol Kassera and hooked by Beth Morris, Naperville, Illinois, 2012. CHARLES HICKS

Beth rolled the edges around cording and whipped them with wool yarn. She mounted the piece into a custom-made frame and offered it to her sister as a gift. However, she loved the completed hooked piece so much that she bought a second pattern to hook for her own home.

In the Judges' Words

- *Fantastic background*
- *Like the blocks of color that go from yellows to reds behind the birches*
- *Nice!*

Buckingham

Susan Grant discovered that taking time to finish what others have started can often bring great reward—and lovely rugs. She bought a partially finished rug at the estate sale of Dianne May, a Canadian rug hooker. "Dianne was a McGown teacher and notorious for starting rugs and then putting them away unfinished," she says. "At the sale, I bought *Buckingham*, which had been started in the early 2000s. Dianne had hooked the red roses at one end, a blue and a purple morning glory, and part of a yellow lily in the colors and style of Helen Connelly."

The rug did not come with any wool or dye formulas, so Susan found a picture of Helen's version of *Buckingham* and devised a color plan to finish the rug. "I hoped that by following Dianne's lead and by analyzing the picture I could achieve the colors Helen used." She used Jewel Tones, Primary Fusion, and Majic Carpet formulas for the swatches for the flowers and leaves and a spot dye called Jane's Green which she darkened, for the background. All of the wool was new Dorr wool except for a textured light blue that she used as a base for the spot-dyed background.

Susan's favorite part of the rug is the yellow-and-orange lilies, but she also notes that they were the most challenging part. "I found it hard to pin down the exact colors that Helen used for those flowers," she says. "As a result, I experimented with dyeing yellows, peach values, and a brown/rose swatch until I came up with a combination of colors that worked together."

Susan learned a lot about color through finishing Dianne's work. "I learned to use purple for shadows; to take a color, in this case mauve, and use it in various places to unify the rug; and to mix bits of color from one leaf or flower into a different leaf or flower to add interest and to achieve a kaleidoscope effect."

To finish the rug, Susan whipped the edges and applied binding tape. The completed rug is displayed in a guest bedroom in her home.

SUSAN GRANT
GEORGETOWN, ONTARIO, CANADA

Susan has been hooking rugs since 2004 when she saw the hand-hooked rugs that her friend had finished and thought that she'd like to try the art when she retired. She has hooked 11 rugs to date. Buckingham is her second rug to be featured in Celebration.

In the Judges' Words

- *Good background*
- *Just gorgeous*
- *Background choice really showcases the flowers*

Buckingham, 72"x 44", #3- and 4-cut wool on burlap.
Designed by Jane McGown Flynn and hooked by Susan Grant, Georgetown, Ontario, Canada, 2013. FISHBACK PHOTOGRAPHY

Kepper Fruit Basket

Natasha Chan enjoys all types of rug hooking, from finely shaded realistic animals to hand-torn primitives and everything in between. "I don't want to exclude anything because there is a reason and a place for it all," she says.

This pattern came to Natasha's attention because she had been wanting to hook some large-scale shaded fruit. "When I happened upon this pattern at a teacher's workshop, I knew I had to hook it," she said.

Natasha chose the colors for the fruits on her own, but she asked workshop teacher Carrie Martin for some help with the background because she knew she wanted a rich, jewel-toned look. To achieve that look, Natasha overdyed as-is textures for the background. By pulling in colors from the fruit and hooking in squiggly lines, she created just the type of rich background that she envisioned.

The basket and the pineapple were also hooked with as-is textures. The fruits are hooked with a mixture of textured wool, natural wool, and wools that had been spot dyed, dip dyed, and marbleized. By using an outline-and-fill technique, Natasha created the dimensional and colorful look she wanted for the fruit. The grapes and the pear stand out as her favorites. "Both have a richness of colors and a realism that I find appealing," she says.

The one fruit that gave her a problem during the hooking was the blue plum beside the pineapple. "It started out as a peach, got lost beside the pineapple, then became a plum, which turned out to be too dark for the background," she says. "It was three efforts and lots of reverse hooking to get it to be passable."

Natasha finished the rug with a whipped edge and a cotton binding. "This is my mother's rug now. She claimed it pretty early on," Natasha says.

NATASHA CHAN
CARMEL, INDIANA

Natasha tried knitting, painting, beading, quilting, and scrapbooking before she looked under her feet to find inspiration in her mom's hooked rugs. She has hooked an estimated "few dozen" rugs. Kepper Fruit Basket is her third rug to be featured in Celebration.

In the Judges' Words

- *Wonderful use of colors against dull basket*
- *Very artsy*
- *Beautiful; bold and rich colors*

Kepper Fruit Basket, 39" x 27", hand-torn strips on linen. Designed by Jane McGown Flynn and hooked by Natasha Chan, Carmel, Indiana, 2013. DAVID CHAN

Cherwell

Judith Ann Davies loves the variety that rug hooking offers. "I've tried most styles and techniques and enjoy them all," she says. "I've never felt a need to settle on one cut or technique, although I do perhaps work more with #4- to 6-cut wool strips."

For her most recent project, Judith wanted to try a William Morris design. "I've always admired his work and his philosophy," she says. "*Cherwell* offered such a variety of flowers and leaves that I thought it would be fun to do, and I was right—it certainly was!"

Judith devised her own color plan and tweaked it a bit during a workshop taught by Ingrid Hieronimus. Many of the swatches she used in this project were dyed by and purchased from Ingrid; however, she also used swatches, over dyes, spot dyes, and dip dyes that she had dyed herself. She rounded out her color scheme with a broad selection of as-is wools from her stash. "I learned to be a little more adventurous and playful in choosing colors while hooking *Cherwell*," she says. "It seemed to want to have a bit of fun!"

Judith enjoyed hooking the little flowers. "They are my favorite part of the rug," she says. "Each was so different and they were all pure fun to hook." The most challenging part of the rug was hooking the turnovers of the larger leaves. She used a #6 cut for those spots, which she admits may have been just a little to big. But after a fair amount of

taking loops out and putting them back in, she was happy with the result.

Judith had planned from the beginning for this to be a floor rug, so she finished it with a hemp rope core covered with a whipped binding. She covered the exposed edge with rug tape to match the color of the rug's background. The finished rug graces the floor in her guest bedroom.

In the Judges' Words

- *Love the use of dip dyes*
- *Like the use of textured wool*
- *Good use of color; nothing jarring*

JUDITH ANN DAVIES
DARTMOUTH, NOVA SCOTIA, CANADA

Judith Ann became intrigued with rug hooking when a neighbor invited her over to see her mother's latest hooked rug. Dorothy Hoban not only showed her how to hook, but also gave her a hoop, pattern, hook, and wool. Judith Ann has completed more than 50 rugs, and Cherwell is her first rug to be featured in Celebration.

Cherwell, 30" x 45", #4-, 5-, and 6-cut wool flannel on linen. William Morris design adapted for rug hooking by Christine Little and hooked by Judith Ann Davies, Dartmouth, Nova Scotia, Canada, 2013. RICHARD GILBERT

Cow Lady Sampler

Sue-Anne Jay had seen this rug design in *RHM* and happened to be at the ATHA Biennial in Lancaster, Pennsylvania, in 2011 where pattern maker Susan Quicksall was a vendor. She had a hard time deciding whether to hook *Cow Lady Sampler* or *Courting Sampler*. She enjoyed her choice so much that she says she may just have to hook *Courting Sampler* in the future.

Sue-Anne based the colors for her rug somewhat loosely on the colors that Susan used in her original rug. "I love bright colors and lots of contrast," she says. "I knew I wanted a brighter version." She used many different techniques, including dip dyes, transitional dyes, swatches, and overdyeing, to create the many colors for her rug. "All of the wool is new with the exception of the navy blue border," she says. "I overdyed navy blue Pendleton skirts for that part of the rug."

Sue-Anne was able to use some leftover wool that she had tossed aside as an almost lost cause. "The wool used for the vine was dyed for another project, but it didn't work," she says. "When the project was started, I pulled this wool out of my 'ugly/to be redyed' stash and it worked perfectly—

and I had enough to get all the way around the border! How often does that happen?"

The most challenging part of completing this pattern was to avoid the temptation to use too many colors. "It is a busy rug already," she says, "so I tried to stay within a few color choices. Of course, when I say 'few' that is relative to the size of the rug."

When all was said and done, Sue-Anne learned a very important lesson: "You *can* eat an elephant! A big rug can be finished. Concentrate on the small area that you are working on and you will get it done one loop at a time."

Sue-Anne finished the edges with hand-painted wool whipped around cording and used rug tape to cover the raw edge. The rug is currently in storage but will be placed in a gallery later this year.

In the Judges' Words

- *Great use of brights*
- *Good balance of color on light and dark backgrounds*
- *Beautiful*

SUE-ANNE JAY
MONTAGUE, PRINCE EDWARD ISLAND, CANADA

Sue-Anne learned to hook as a hobby to fill her time during the off-season of her tourist business. She has hooked about 30 rugs plus untold smaller items, including everything from ornaments to tea cozies. Cow Lady Sampler is her first rug to be featured in Celebration.

Cow Lady Sampler, 4' x 5', #3- and 4-cut wool on linen.
Designed by Susan Quicksall and hooked by Sue-Anne Jay, Montague, Prince Edward Island, Canada, 2013. DAN MACKINNON

December Snows

K aren Gaskin enjoys hooking rugs in smaller cuts. "I believe I have more control of the shapes and colors in the rug designs," she says. "Many of my art pieces are of nature and landscapes, and I approach each new design with a painter's eye."

That painter's eye was especially helpful in this rendition of *December Snows*. "*December Snows* is a beautiful and challenging winter scene," she says. "I have a preference for peaceful country and farm settings."

Karen color planned the piece with the help of her teacher, who suggested a plaid for the evergreen and helped her to choose the colors for the center tree from her own wool stash. Karen chose the color palette for the rest of the rug. She hooked spot-dyed wool for the snow and used dyed swatches in many places throughout the rug. She used as-is wools in the evergreen and in the clouds. "Much of my wool stash is recycled wool clothing," she says. "The challenge of the hunt for beautiful wool to reuse is exhilarating, not to mention a cost savings."

Karen enjoyed figuring out how to hook the large tree in the foreground. "That central tree is my favorite part of the rug," she says. "Using different shades of brown and hooking in irregular lines gave the tree movement and an arboreal character."

She notes that the open expanses of snow and sky were especially challenging. "I wanted those large spaces to have interest for the viewer," she says. "Adding the moon and the horizon clouds enhanced the sky. And hooking a moon enabled me to add shadows and highlights in the snow."

Through hooking this rug, Karen learned that plaid is a very versatile and useful wool for a pictorial rug. "For me, plaid is an underused resource better suited to primitive rugs," she says. "But I was very pleased with the look of the clouds, which were hooked in a periwinkle and white plaid. They suggest the cold cirrus clouds of a winter night."

Karen whipped the rolled edge with wool yarn. The completed rug is displayed in her guest bedroom.

KAREN GASKIN
JEFFERSON, MASSACHUSETTS

When Karen's mother-in-law passed away, her rug hooking frame was handed down to Karen. Soon after, Karen ordered a rug hooking kit to try out what always struck her as a fascinating art. She has hooked six rugs in the past five years. December Snows is her first rug to be featured in Celebration.

In the Judges' Words

- *Very nice interpretation*
- *Shadows bring this to life*
- *Fabulous tree*

December Snows, 36" x 24", #3- and 4-cut wool on burlap. Designed by Joan Moshimer and hooked by Karen Gaskin, Jefferson, Massachusetts, 2013.

Eagle

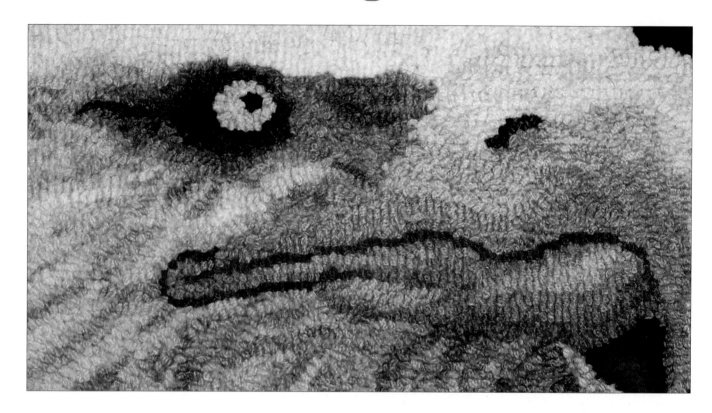

Erika Decree hooked this rug as a surprise Christmas gift for her husband. "He is a retired Army officer and the eagle is symbolic of our great country," she says. "Here in Montana, we see bald eagles on a daily basis, hunting and soaring in thermals."

Erika color planned the rug and dyed most of the wool. For the white portion of the eagle, she used a 10-value swatch over Dorr white wool.

The eye is Erika's favorite part of this rug. "I learned from Judy Carter to hook the eyes first," she says. "Once the eye was hooked, the eagle told me how to do the rest." One of the most difficult areas to hook was the eagle's head. "Getting the subtle variations in the white so there would be depth and dimension was a challenge," she says. "I used a color photo of an eagle in a similar position." One important lesson she learned from hooking this rug was to trust that a 10-value swatch has enough variation in values to achieve the results she wanted.

Erika needed about four or five months to complete the rug, but since it was a Christmas present, she had to limit her rug hooking sessions to times when her husband was not home.

To finish the rug, Erika whipstitched the edges with yarn in a similar color. The rug currently hangs on the wall in the family room with several other American and military-themed pictures, paintings, and rugs.

In the Judges' Words

- *Good use of contrasts within the same colors*
- *Eagle comes right off the page*
- *Lettering and background eye-catching*

ERIKA DECREE
WHITEFISH, MONTANA

In 2005, Erika's mother finally convinced her daughter to try rug hooking. "Try it, you'll like it" bore true. Since then Erika notes that she's hooked too many rugs to count, but possibly close to 150. Eagle is her third rug to be featured in Celebration.

Eagle, 26" x 18", #3-cut wool on rug warp. Designed by Leonard Feenan and hooked by Erika DeCree, Whitefish, Montana, 2013.

Geese in Flight

Tatiana Knodel fell in love with this rug when she saw the finished piece that had been hooked by a member of her rug hooking group. "I couldn't sleep well until I found and bought the pattern," she says. "I was drawn to this pattern because of its straight lines. The straight lines are a powerful motif in this design. They define the entire rug, from the sunlight in the sky and the shoreline to the birds in the sky."

Tatiana color planned the rug herself. "The original rug was hooked in black, brown, gray, yellow, and white—a color scheme that didn't appeal to me," she says. "As soon as I saw the pattern, I had a mental picture of what I wanted the final rug to look like. I just pulled the pieces from my considerable stash of wool until I was happy with the combination."

Tatiana used only new Dorr wool; no dyed wool was used. The sky with its rays of sun is Tatiana's favorite part of the rug because it was a challenging and interesting spot to place color.

The most challenging part of the rug was hooking the straight lines, so Tatiana developed a special sculpturing technique. "In order to make the lines straight, I first hooked the lines in the usual way, and then I shaped the last line with scissors," she says. "The scissors must be sharp and should be held vertically. I only cut those loops that are not right on the straight line." Tatiana uses this technique for almost all the lines in her rugs, even if they

Geese in Flight, 53" x 28", #3-cut wool on burlap. Designed by Thor Hansen and hooked by Tatiana Knodel, Sudbury, Ontario, Canada, 2012.

are not straight. "When I do this in pictures of animals, people, or flowers, then everything will have a well-defined outer contour," she says.

To finish the rug, Tatiana whipped the edges with wool yarn so that the stitching was barely visible and finished the rug with binding tape. The completed rug hangs on the wall in her living room.

TATIANA KNODEL
SUDBURY, ONTARIO, CANADA

Tatiana jumped into rug hooking with both feet when she attended a rug hooking group meeting in her hometown with a friend. She has hooked 18 rugs and 23 wall hangings in the past five years. Geese in Flight is her first rug to be featured in Celebration.

Harvest Fair

For a fall celebration rug, *Harvest Fair* has all the trimmings—and Janet Boates couldn't agree more.

The turkey that dominates the rug is surrounded by a selection of colorful, delicately shaded fall fruits and vegetables. The border completes the rug with a cascading line of fall leaves and acorns. Janet decided to hook this rug not only because of its subject, but also because she thought the pattern would be challenging.

Janet color planned the rug and dyed the wool using spot dyes and swatches. She picked colors based on the realistic colors of a turkey and commonly available fall seasonal vegetables. She finds that realistic images and colors appeal more to her than other choices.

Janet points to the corn as her favorite part of the rug. "I used a wider #7 cut here, while in the rest of the rug I used a #4 cut, so the corn really stands out. I also enjoyed hooking the fruit and vegetables because I wanted the challenge of shading them."

"The turkey was the most challenging part of the rug because I had no picture to refer to and it was very detailed," she says. "I was constantly thumbing through magazines and pictures to find the exact turkey that I wanted to hook. Finally, I settled on two pictures and my own imagination."

Janet found that she learned one set of quotes patience and perseverance through hooking this rug. "This was a challenging piece, and I would hook a little bit each day and leave it on a chair overnight. The next morning I would get up and eye it critically and maybe rip some of it out or decide to change the color of some area. Eventually, I was able to achieve the look I wanted."

Janet whipped the edges to finish the rug. The completed rug is displayed in her family room in the fall.

JANET BOATES
KINGS COUNTY,
NOVA SCOTIA, CANADA

Janet Boate's friends persuaded her to take a rug hooking course with them at a local community hall. That was four years ago, and to date she has hooked 40 rugs and wall hangings. Harvest Fair *is her first rug to be featured in* Celebration.

Harvest Fair, 34" x 38", #3-, 4-, and 7-cut new and recycled wool on burlap.
Designed by Christine Little and hooked by Janet Boates, Kings County, Nova Scotia, Canada, 2013. PAUL DESPRES

In the Judges' Words

- *The border makes this rug*
- *Nice shading*
- *Great fruits and vegetables*

Hereke

Martha Beals works best when she has several projects on the go at once. "I enjoy having numerous different rugs going at one time to keep me involved in all techniques and to challenge me," she says.

In *Hereke*, Martha certainly found a challenge. "I fell in love with this design a long time ago after a lecture by Sally Ballinger," she says. "I bought the pattern then and kept pulling it out but never had a good color plan."

Martha's definition of a good color plan for this rug centered on finding the perfect red. "I knew I wanted red in the rug and dyed until I found the right red. Then I dyed that formula over six different colored wools in the swatch method." With the help of her teacher, Betty McClentic, Martha worked through what other colors were needed and why.

Martha added green, red's complement, to the color palette. Then she added golds and a swatch that goes from light green to red. The background is a deep red wool spot dyed with the red, greens, and golds that are found in the rug. Last, she added a plaid that incorporated all the same colors.

Martha needed about two and a half years to finish this rug, but following her usual method of work, she paused here and there to hook a couple smaller rugs for her grandchildren.

In hooking this rug, Martha discovered a number of things about working with color, including the importance of balancing colors. "I see this rug as 'red' because that was the most intensive dyeing and I love that color," she says. "But many people do not see the red because it is well balanced with its complement." She also learned to use a swatch equally to balance the rug.

Martha folded the edges forward and whipped them with 100% wool yarn dyed to match the background. The rug is displayed over a section of railing in her multilevel home.

MARTHA BEALS
SIDNEY, MAINE

In 1993, Martha sold her retail business and was looking for something creative to fill her time. She found rug hooking at a county fair. Since then she has hooked more than 40 rugs and a number of smaller projects. Hereke is her first rug to be featured in Celebration.

Hereke, 68" x 40", #3- and 4-cut wool flannel strips on 2 x 2 cotton backing. Designed by Jane McGown Flynn and hooked by Martha Beals, Sidney, Maine, 2013. BRIANA WOLGEMUTH

Kyoto

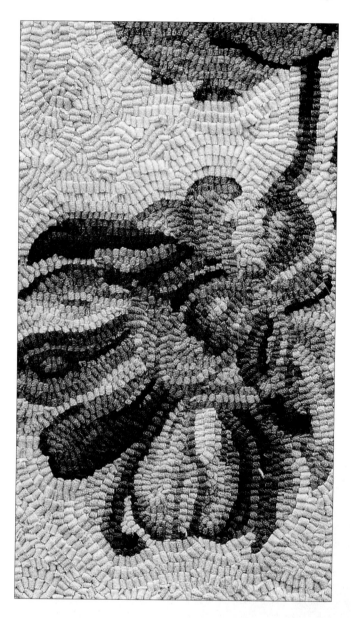

L ouise Royka Gleason has been developing a technique over the past few years to use multiple colors to produce an effect. "I listen to what the rug is telling me, where I feel it wants me to go with color and image," she says. "*Kyoto* is an example of this technique. It seems to just come naturally. I feel there is a rhythm to hooking which combines movement, color, image, and a place of mind."

Louise chose this pattern because she thought it would be a good fit for her skills. She also liked the flow of the design. The flowers and their leaves move gracefully up and down the rug, leading the eye easily from one open blossom to the next. The one question she gets quite often is about the characters in the border of the rug. "I checked with the designer last year," she says. "The symbols mean absolutely nothing. I also asked the designers about the yin/yang in one of the corners (it is inverted). No special meaning there either."

Choosing a color scheme to fit the rug was a little more difficult. "It took me a while to decide on the colors," she says. "I had many suggestions. In the end I chose colors from an invitation from the Worcester Art Museum." Jeanne Benjamin provided the French vanilla–colored wool for the background plus swatches and spot dyes and worked with Louise to put the colors together.

The leaves were a big challenge for Louise. She found she needed patience and a willingness to take a chance with colors to make them work. But once the rug was finished, Louise appreciated how the colors came together to create the leaves. "The use of multiple colors to achieve the look I wanted was very satisfying."

Louise finds finishing a rug to be difficult, and she is constantly working to improve her technique. For this rug, she whipped the edges over cotton cord, mitered the edges, and covered the raw edge of the backing with binding tape. The completed rug is displayed in a bedroom where its colors complement the walls.

In the Judges' Words

- *The leaves are so lifelike; they really carry the composition*
- *Excellent use of color*

LOUISE ROYKA GLEASON
WORCESTER, MASSACHUSETTS

Louise had no idea what a hooked rug was until she attended Jeanne Benjamin's rug hooking show with a friend at the nearby Salem Cross Inn. That visit inspired her to start hooking rugs when she retired 15 years ago. She has hooked nearly 50 pieces, and Kyoto is her third piece to be featured in Celebration.

Kyoto, 4'10" x 3'5", #3-, 4-, 5-, and 6-cut dyed wool on linen.
Designed by Rittermere-Hurst-Field and hooked by Louise Royka Gleason, Worcester, Massachusetts, 2013. JEREMIAH BENJAMIN

Paisley Hex

Rosalie Powell was attracted to this paisley design because she owns a collection of antique paisley shawls. Hooking a rug with the motifs was a way for her to share her enthusiasm for their unique style. This rug also falls squarely within the type of rugs she likes to hook: finely-shaded flowers, fruit, and scrolls.

To plan the colors, Rosalie turned to her antique shawl collection. One of the shawls there provided the color scheme for this rug. For Rosalie, the source of those colors gave the rug an air of authenticity.

Rosalie used dip dyes, spot dyes, and a swatch for the scrolls. The gold and navy were off-the-bolt wool, and the background was hooked with a spot dye by Angela Foote. In addition to new wool, Rosalie also hooked pieces of an antique shawl that had been damaged.

The inner border and part of the scroll that were made from the antique paisley shawl are Rosalie's favorite parts of the rug. But using the antique shawl was a challenge. The strips had to be cut with the threads, lengthwise, to keep the strips from unraveling. She started cutting them by hand but soon learned that she could use a #8 cutter.

Rosalie paid special attention to the symmetry of the rug, making sure that not only the motifs were mirror images, but also the colors. The rug is in symmetry from top to bottom and left to right. The paisleys are not symmetrical individually, but the other elements are. That lack of symmetry within the individual paisley motifs as well as the vivid blue color make the paisleys stand out and give them added interest.

Hooking this rug gave Rosalie a chance to delve deeper into the history of antique paisley shawls, which in turn led her to give a presentation to the local antique club.

Rosalie whipped the edges over cording to finish the rug, taking extra care with the unusual number of sides for a rug. The completed rug is displayed in her studio.

ROSALIE H. POWELL
WEST TISBURY, MASSACHUSETTS

Rosalie's mother taught her to hook rugs at eight years old when she wanted to enter a hooked chair seat in the 4-H exhibit. She returned to hooking on her own in the 1970s and has completed 78 rugs and small pieces in the decades since. Paisley Hex is her third rug to be featured in Celebration.

In the Judges' Words

- *Excellent*
- *One's eye moves around the rug with ease*
- *Outstanding color choices*

Paisley Hex, 53" x 34", #3-cut wool and antique paisley shawl on burlap.
Designed by Jane McGown Flynn and hooked by Rosalie H. Powell, West Tisbury, Massachusetts, 2013. LISA BROWN

Square Harmony

Jill Hicks was first drawn to this pattern when she saw it pictured in *Celebration XXI*. "I really liked the combination of the floral and geometric pattern—and the added plus was having birds in the design," she says. "That *Celebration* rug was done with a light background. However, after some consideration, I decided that I wanted to try hooking a dark background."

Jill was unable to find an example of this pattern hooked with a dark background, so she consulted with several rug hooking teachers and a handful of friends for input and ideas. When she was done gathering information—and after some trial and error—she planned a color scheme that took into consideration all the advice but still suited her tastes.

The dark background was hooked from recycled wool purchased at local resale shops. The colored fabrics were a combination of new wool off the bolt, recycled wool, and hand-dyed wool. Jill mixed and matched dye techniques, focusing more on the resulting color than the method of dyeing.

Jill found the most frustrating part of hooking this rug to be the middle geometric portion of the design. "I had decided that I could not hook that part of the rug until I knew what colors I was going to use in the floral design because I felt the two had to be tied together with similar colors," she says. So she proceeded to hook all of the floral section, leaving the geometrics until later. When she tried to hook the geometrics with the same colors, the sections competed against each other. She finally ended up hooking the geometric portion with muted variations of the flower colors and hooked a simpler pattern in the squares.

Overall, Jill is pleased with the way the geometrics and the florals work together, and she likes the dark background. She finished the rug with a strip of wool cut on the bias and hand sewn in place. The completed rug is on display in the foyer where it gets little foot traffic.

In the Judges' Words

- *Love the roughness of the hooking in this piece*
- *Exciting, rich color*
- *Color choices are balanced; nothing jumps out*

JILL HICKS
VALPARAISO, INDIANA

Jill started hooking rugs after her husband gave her a Christmas gift that included a trip to the Green Mountain Rug Hooking School in Vermont. In the three years since, she has hooked three rugs. Square Harmony is her first rug to be featured in Celebration.

Square Harmony, 54" x 34", #6- and 8-cut recycled, hand-dyed, and off-the-bolt wool on linen.
Designed by Monika Jones and hooked by Jill Hicks, Valparaiso, Indiana, 2013. WALT BUKVA

St. Nicholas with Cardinal

Starr Burgess chose this pattern to hook for one simple reason: "Santa's face makes me smile." His face made her smile even more as she made small alterations to the pattern to add her own touch to the composition of this rug. She added glasses inching down Santa's nose and added some special three-dimensional effects with a variety of hooking techniques.

Starr needed only two weeks to hook this piece. She started with a kit and made it into a pillow. All the materials she needed, even the pre–color planned and dyed wool selections, were included in the kit. Having everything ready to go gave Starr time to focus on bringing the rug to life with some inventive and creative additions.

"I viewed this pillow as a clay artist adding clay, but I did it with hooking, building up the wool with shaping, and in many shades of wool, just like a painter adds colors to a canvas," she said. "The more I hooked, the more it drew me into hooking greater depth of wool and colors."

Starr hooked the nose and eyes first. After she completed

STARR BURGESS
IDA, MICHIGAN

A hooked footstool on display at Sauder Village three years ago tempted Starr to start rug hooking herself. In the past four years—which includes time off to nurse a broken wrist—she has hooked four pieces. This is her first rug to be featured in Celebration.

St. Nicholas with Cardinal, 18" x 18", #3- to 7-cut wool on linen.
Designed by Tish Murphy and hooked by Starr Burgess, Ida, Michigan, 2013.

the face, she added the beard and hair by twisting the wool and adding highs and lows to get the effect of hair in different shades of whites and grays.

Starr worked with the wool to bring even more dimension to the bird and the staff and Santa's outfit. "Mind you, I don't know the rules of rug hooking or what I should or shouldn't do," she said, "so I just added where my eyes told

me to add more. As this was going to be my pillow, I knew I had to bring Santa alive. When I sit across the room, I wanted it to draw my eyes with the dimensions."

Starr finished the piece with piping covered by wool that matched the colors in the hooking. Starr's Santa pillow sits on her checked couch in the living room year-round where it awaits visits from family and friends.

Sunflowers

Connie Bradley enjoys hooking wider cut rugs, and she especially enjoys wide cut shading techniques. And when spring and summer roll around, she likes to hook "cheery" rugs to celebrate the seasons. This pattern, *Sunflowers*, incorporates lots of shading in the flowers and the leaves and it fits Connie's "cheery" criteria, making it an appealing pattern.

Connie planned the colors. She used the typical yellows and golds for the sunflowers, but she chose purples for the morning glories to provide a complement to the yellow

sunflowers. She used swatches, dip dyes, and textures to hook this rug. She chose recycled wool for the flower centers and the background. For the morning glories, she used a dip dye. She hooked the wood grain–like border with a textured wool.

Her favorite parts of this rug are the petals of the sunflowers. She was able to use different values, starting with light in the foreground of a flower and moving to dark in the receding petals, to give each flower the illusion of depth. Then within each petal, she planned the shading to move from light on the outer edges of the petal to dark within.

Connie feels that the solid blue background makes the shaded flowers and leaves pop, but she also found that the background was the most difficult part of the rug for her to hook. The relatively large expanse needed to be filled in

Sunflowers, 34¹/₂" x 39", #5- and 6-cut wool on linen.
Designed by Fraser and hooked by Connie Bradley, Wellington, Ohio, 2013.

carefully, and while she didn't hook in straight lines, she did need to employ some regularity to keep the background even so it wouldn't distract from the flowers.

The wood grain–like border of the rug incorporates a bit of movement. Connie added the slight variation in the line to find a happy balance between keeping the border "straight" but also giving it the wavy look of true wood grain. Using longer strips of the textured material helped Connie to achieve this impression.

Connie finished the rug with a herringbone stitch. The completed rug is on display in her living room.

CONNIE BRADLEY
WELLINGTON, OHIO

Connie learned to hook rugs 26 years ago from her mother. Counting everything from rugs to table mats, Connie estimates that she's hooked about 100 pieces. Sunflowers is her second rug to be featured in Celebration.

Turkish Primitive

K ate LeMasters chose this rug pattern because she was interested in hooking a Turkish rug design using textured wools. Kate finds the symmetry of design and the contrast with the horizontal rows of the background appealing in this style of rug.

When she started to color plan the rug, she knew she wanted to use red, blue, gold, and cream. Anita White helped her to fine-tune the color scheme. A few of the pieces of wool were dyed, but the majority of the wool was as-is in light/dark prints and plaids. Kate hooked mottled hand-dyed red and blues to mimic the tonal color changes in those areas of the rug.

The more vivid blues hooked in rows in the center of the rug contrast against the darker colors hooked along the edges. That added contrast adds interest to the rug and catches a viewer's eye. The easy symmetry of the rug is comforting and offers a balance that seems to reach out and touch the viewer.

Overall, Kate is pleased with the finished rug. "I love the authentic Turkish colors," she says. "I also love the look of hooking it all in horizontal rows." That style is a telltale sign of a Turkish rug and that identifier, combined with the

typical colors, give Kate a great feeling of accomplishment. Kate notes that the most challenging parts of the rug were the squares in the inner border of the rug. She found it difficult to keep the squares aligned and needed to hook extra cautiously in those areas.

Kate finished the rug with a wool facing. The edges are corded and whipped. She used a purchased and preassembled 4" fringe made from 100% wool on the two short ends of the completed rug. The rug is currently on display in her family room.

KATE LeMASTERS
RAYMORE, MISSOURI

Kate was inspired to learn to hook rugs after she found her mother's old hook from the 1940s. Kate started hooking rugs in 2006 and has hooked well over 60 rugs since then. Turkish Primitive is her first rug to be featured in Celebration.

*Turkish Primitive, 56" x 32",
#6-cut wool on linen. Designed by
Jane McGown Flynn and hooked
by Kate LeMasters, Raymore,
Missouri, 2013.* PEARCE PHOTOGRAPHY

In the Judges' Words

- *Stunning color combination*
- *Nice, crisp corners of motifs*
- *Beautifully finished*

Biscuits Lefévre-Utile

Cyndra Mogayzel has always loved art nouveau posters and was inspired to hook one of her own after seeing Lissa Williamson's Art Nouveau Poster Rug at a nearby rug hooking exhibit. The idea for her own work didn't come together until she attended the ATHA Biennial in Lancaster, Pennsylvania, when she and several friends had lunch out at a restaurant decorated with art nouveau posters.

"We liked them so much that we decided to do a group project for the class we would be taking with Ingrid Hieronimus at the Ocean Shores Rug School the following spring," she says. "We each picked a different poster to adapt."

Lissa helped Cyndra adapt the poster for rug hooking, and Ingrid dyed the wool. "I felt that capturing the feel of the poster required the limited palette that would have been used for printing it in 1897," Cyndra says. Cyndra also recreated the lettering from the poster, using two colors to form each letter. The black forms the main body of the letter while gold that is used elsewhere in the rug highlights the letter and gives it more dimension.

Cyndra says getting the perspective correct was a challenge because she had to work in a limited palette that comprised basically all neutrals. "The poster has three planes: the girl, the frame, and the field in the background," she says. "The most difficult part was getting the background that she is sitting on to not change the perspective on her body. It was fairly easy to do the dark under where she is sitting; it was very difficult to do the lighter part by her lower leg and still keep the field in the distance." Cyndra saved that part of the rug for last and took great care to get it right, spending nearly a week on a section that amounted to essentially a dozen strips.

To keep the feel of a poster, Cyndra framed the finished rug. She is pleased with the results and displays the rug on the wall of her living room.

CYNDRA MOGAYZEL
ANNAPOLIS, MARYLAND

Cyndra became interested in hooking rugs after attending a beginning rug class by Jane Halliwell Green. In the six years since, she has hooked eight rugs, six pillows, and one wall hanging and regularly attends rug hooking workshops. Her rug's inclusion in Celebration *marks her first rug hooking award.*

In the Judges' Words

- *Great color combinations*
- *Lettering reads well*
- *Good interpretation of art nouveau style*

Biscuits Lefévre-Utile by Alphonse Mucha, 18″ x 24¹/₂″, #2- and 3-cut hand-dyed wool swatches on monk's cloth. Adapted by Lissa Williamson, with permission, from an art nouveau poster and hooked by Cyndra Mogayzel, Annapolis, Maryland, 2013. PHOTO BY PETER MOGAYZEL

Carousel

Pat Stangeland enjoys the creativity she finds in rug hooking. With the creative freedom to go in so many directions, she rarely has trouble coming up with a subject that will pique her interest. *Carousel* is a confluence of her surroundings.

"I was thinking about a design that I could hook at the Cambria Pines Rug Camp that would take advantage of Eric Sandberg's expertise in color planning," she says. "At the same time, my husband, Tim, and daughter, Shannon, were restoring an antique carousel horse. Reminded of the artistry of the talented woodcarvers who created the beautiful animals, I decided to design a rug that would celebrate their contribution to our world."

The carousel menagerie that Pat designed was based on animals carved for early 20th century carousels. She found some of the drawings in Dover's pictorial archives

publications and used others with permission from *Carving Carousel Animals* (Sterling, 2008). She drew the remainder of the animals from public domain pictures of period carousel animals.

Pat tapped into Eric's knowledge of color, and they worked with the drawings to come up with swatches to take to Cambria Pines. Once together at camp, they combined their swatches to come up with the final plan. The animals were primarily hooked from 6- to 8-value swatches with a small amount of spot-dyed wool. The background wool is broken up with a fun confetti effect that Pat achieved by randomly placing loops of colors that were used to hook the carousel animals.

Pat finished the rug with binding tape. The completed rug graces the floor of her guest room—the only room in the house where her six dogs dare not go.

Carousel, 55½" diameter, #3-cut with some #2- and 4-cut wool on rug warp. Adapted, with permission, from carousel drawings and photographs and hooked by Pat Stangeland, Montesano, Washington, 2013.

In the Judges' Words

- Excellent use of complementary colors
- Beautifully hooked
- This is a masterful piece, well executed

PAT STANGELAND
MONTESANO, WASHINGTON

Pat was first exposed to rug hooking during her career as an occupational therapist with the California Children Services. She never used it in her professional life, but was delighted to pick it up as a hobby 17 years ago. She has hooked more than 50 rugs. Carousel is her third rug to be featured in Celebration.

Northern Flicker

For as long as she can remember, Dianne Warren has been involved in some sort of fiber craft. From sewing and quilting to tatting and spinning, Dianne can always find something to learn, and then she usually finds ways to incorporate at least some of those techniques into her hooked mats.

Northern Flicker includes elements from Dianne's forays into embroidery and beading. "*Northern Flicker* is primarily wool fabric," she says. "However, near the bottom is a series of silver beading wires with seed beads and cotton embroidery floss. The floss is tied into tassels and strung onto the wire, separated by beads." The resulting effect is a three-dimensional evergreen branch upon which the flicker is perched.

Dianne designed the flicker to fill an inset in the wall of her cottage. She created most of the colors in the flicker and tree needles from jar-dyed swatches. She used leftover spot-dyed worms for the tree and the stems, and some off-the-bolt wool for small amounts of color. "I purchased the background gray/blue from Jon Ciemiewicz, which was likely a wandering technique, and was just what I was looking for," she says.

The most difficult part of this project was hooking the black spots on the body. "First I hooked them where I thought they should be," she says, "then hooked the surrounding area. They were mostly hooked as two tails of wool. Later, I pulled out and re-hooked many, squeezing them in where they would fit and look good. I probably should have just put them in last."

Dianne needed a unique finishing option because of the mat's odd shape and its position on the cabin wall, so she asked her husband to cut a piece of plywood to fit the inset in the wall. She then used staples to anchor the corners to the back of the board. She stretched the linen horizontally and vertically with a lacing of cotton twine until the piece fit snuggly.

She now plans to hook a companion mat featuring a downy woodpecker.

DIANNE WARREN
ST. JOHN'S, NEWFOUNDLAND, CANADA

Dianne first picked up a rug hooking tool in a Chetticamp trivet kit in 1976 but didn't find the time to really delve into the art until 2004, the year after she retired. She has hooked more than 100 pieces—17 of those are room-sized and all of them are photographed—and owns Atlantic Rug Hooking Supplies. This is her first rug to appear in Celebration.

In the Judges' Words

- *A beautifully realistic bird*
- *Love the eyelash fringe in the pine tree*
- *Nicely done*

Northern Flicker, 10¹/₂″ x 20″, #3- and 4-cut wool on linen. Adapted from a photograph from Cornell Lab of Ornithology and hooked by Dianne Warren, St. John's, Newfoundland, Canada 2013.

Grandma

J an Grose first saw the sepia photograph upon which her rug is based when she was 16. "I knew I wanted to hook it," she says. "Grandma's impishness and playfulness, even when she was in her 90s, is so evident in this photo. When I learned that Donna Hrkman was teaching at Sauder Village, I knew this was the perfect opportunity to learn Donna's monochromatic portrait techniques."

Jan dyed all the wool for the project. "I'm kind of a purist about fabric," she says. "I pulled bits and pieces out of my stash that may have been recycled, but it's primarily new wool dyed just for this project." She based her color plan on the one established by the photographer and dyed wool in a wide variety of shades of sepia. She had to make several attempts to get the right color, but during the hooking process, she found that many of the colors she had rejected became useful in developing detail and contrast in small areas.

Her favorite part of this rug is her grandmother's face. Jan worked hard to capture her flirty expression and was pleased to see it shine through in the hooked piece. "The process started with drawing the portrait on linen. A number of steps were involved, including scanning the photo and enlarging it to the actual size of the rug," she says. "Using monochromatic colors—getting enough detail while using just one color—was a challenge. There was a lot of trial and error. Hooking, removing, and hooking again."

One lesson Jan learned from hooking this rug is that faces are funny—figuratively and literally. "I learned that making minor changes can make a major difference," she says.

Jan finished the rug by turning the extra linen toward the right side and whipping the edge with wool yarn. The completed rug will hang in her home.

JAN GROSE
PLAIN CITY, OHIO

Despite starting out on the wrong foot with burlap from a chain store, unknown fabric, and the notion that rug hooking would be an inexpensive hobby, Jan enjoyed rug hooking so much that she has hooked more than 40 rugs in the past 15 years. She co-owns a rug hooking business called Roche Riverhouse. Grandma is her second rug to be featured in Celebration.

In the Judges' Words

- *Shadows are extraordinarily well done*
- *Purple accents elevated the monochromatic color scheme*
- *Great sepia tones*

Grandma, 22″ x 31″, #4-cut on linen. Adapted from a circa 1915 family photo and hooked by Jan Grose, Plain City, Ohio, 2013.

Hansel and Gretel

Katy Powell's current rug hooking projects all center around one theme: good versus evil as depicted in children's fairy tales. Her rendition of *Hansel and Gretel* is based on a drawing by Arthur Rackham, a famous illustrator who provided the artwork for many English books in the first half of the 20th century.

"When I first looked at the original illustration, I thought it was too detailed to hook," Katy says, "but I loved the expressions of the faces, and Arthur Rackham's illustrations have always been a favorite of mine. Carol Fegles, one of my former teachers, encouraged me to try it."

Katy started the color planning process by first surveying the wool she had on hand. Once she had a good idea of what was in her stash, she color planned the rug with some input from her rug hooking group in Portland. She used both recycled and new wool.

"Part of the 'House Challenge,' a rug hooking contest sponsored by the Oregon ATHA in Spring 2013, was to use a blue and white plaid that was sent to each participant," Katy says. "That swatch was used in the shawls." *Hansel and Gretel* won the challenge.

In hooking this rug, Katy discovered that the use of spot dyes and plaids for the trees and shrubs created a nice look and feel to the leaves and branches. Hooking the witch's face and hands was the most enjoyable part to work on. "I think hooking Gretel's face was the most challenging because it was so small," she said. "I tweaked and re-hooked it numerous times. Hansel and the witch were very easy compared to her."

Katy finishes all of her fairy tale rugs with dark or black wool and adds black wool tabs for a metal rod. "I was displaying my fairy tale rugs on a big wall going up my staircase but recently sold my home," she says. "Maybe by the time this prints I will have a nice big wall to hang my rugs on."

KATY POWELL
PORTLAND, OREGON

Katy came across hooked rugs when she worked with her father in his punch hooking company, Rumpelstiltskin's. She has finished over 200 punched rugs, and since 2002, she has added about 25 hooked rugs to her name. Hansel and Gretel is her second rug to be featured in Celebration.

In the Judges' Words

- *Incredible contrast and execution*
- *Captures the darkness of the moment*
- *Successful interpretation of a classic image*

Hansel and Gretel, 21" x 26¹/₂", #3- and 4-cut wool on monk's cloth.
Adapted, with permission, from an illustration by Arthur Rackham and hooked by Katy Powell, Portland, Oregon, 2012. OWEN CAREY

Jack Rides

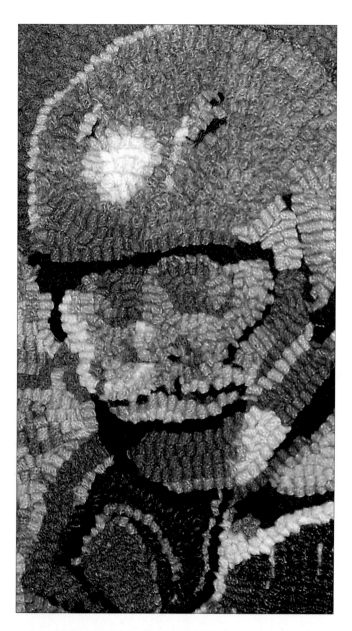

Carla was looking for a gift idea for her husband that would commemorate his years of riding a motorcycle, an activity he has enjoyed competitively and for his own entertainment since age 11. "I had this picture of him riding at Sonoma Raceway and was planning on taking a portrait class from Laura Pierce," she says. "I sent the picture to Laura and she did her magic in Photoshop and enlarged the photo on linen."

Carla was working from a photograph that she liked and she wanted to stay true to the colors in the picture. Input from Laura at the portrait class got her started, and a trip down to Gene Shepherd's First Saturday filled in some big holes. "I wish you could have seen us going through every piece of wool Gene had on his shelves trying to find just the right shades and chroma," she says. "Funny thing was I purchased the wool then let it sit on the table in Gene's studio. We had to drive back out from Long Beach to Anaheim to pick it up!"

Carla used primarily new wool with some recycled wool, including an old wool suit in her closet that she tore up late one night to get the perfect gray. Many of the wools were dyed with dip, spot, and dump dyes. She also used Gene's dyeing-without-dye technique to lighten the value on several of the colors used in the rug.

Completing her husband's face was the most difficult yet most rewarding part of hooking this rug. "The face was the place where I started and what I agonized over the most," she says. "Everyone who knows my husband says it looks like him, so all the reverse hooking done on this section was worthwhile."

Carla finished the rug by folding the linen to the back, pinning the tape in place, and then whipping the edge and attaching the tape at the same time. After whipping the edge, she stitched the loose edge of the tape to the back of the rug. The completed rug hangs in her husband's home office.

CARLA JENSEN
CLOVIS, CALIFORNIA

A rug hooking class for beginners at a local quilting store got Carla interested in rug hooking; a trip to the Wool Poppies' rug hooking retreat near Yosemite cemented her interest. She has hooked nine pieces in the past five years. Jack Rides is her first rug to be featured in Celebration.

In the Judges' Words

- *Great use of design and color*
- *Contour hooking brings this to life*
- *Rider and his motorcycle are wonderfully executed*

Jack Rides, 36" x 26¼", #3-, 4-, and 5-cut wool on linen. Adapted by Laura Pierce from a photograph by Carla Jensen, Clovis, California, 2013.

Klimt Ottoman

Kim Kaelin likes to incorporate her rugs into functional works of art such as pillows and benches. "I found myself working months on a rug just to roll it up and keep it in the closet," she says. "Creating benches and pillows out of my hooking is a great way to display my work."

Kim combined her appreciation of Klimt's work with her passion for functional art in this piece. "Gustav Klimt's painting *Lady with Fan* is one of my favorites," she says. "For my large bench design, I extracted the fantasy birds and flowers from the background of his painting. The design ended up being large enough to pull in several more birds from Klimt's other works."

Kim gives all the credit for the color planning to the master, Gustav Klimt, himself. She kept a photo of the painting beside her throughout the entire process so she could refer to it during color planning and hooking the rug.

For such a large piece, Kim needed a lot of background wool. "I'm fascinated with colors that are right in between two analogous color groups," she says. "Sometimes I look at the background and it appears lime green. Other times it appears more yellow. To achieve this color, I first dyed natural wool yellow then did a short post dip in a green dye pot."

Kim's favorite parts of working on this rug were the color and the whimsy of the design. "I learned how fun it is to reproduce the work of a master. You can discover so much about an artist's use of color and design when you spend months examining his work," she says.

Kim finished the rug into a bench that was made from

plywood and turned legs. High-density, 5" foam gives the seat its height. From backing to bench, the project took six months to complete. While she often sells her work, Kim decided to keep the completed bench and placed it at the foot of her bed where it makes her smile each time she enters the room.

KIM KAELIN
STILLWATER, MINNESOTA

Kim learned to hook at a beginning rug hooking workshop sponsored by a local quilt shop. She has hooked 50 pieces in the past 10 years. Klimt Ottoman *is her second piece to be featured in Celebration.*

Klimt Ottoman, 71″ x 35″, #8-cut wool on linen. Adapted from Gustav Klimt's Lady with Fan *and hooked by Kim Kaelin, Stillwater, Minnesota, 2013.* SHARON MCKENDRY

In the Judges' Words

- *Unexpected background adds life and whimsy*
- *Delightful use of selected elements of Klimt's painting*
- *Love the color combinations*

Marry Me, Mary

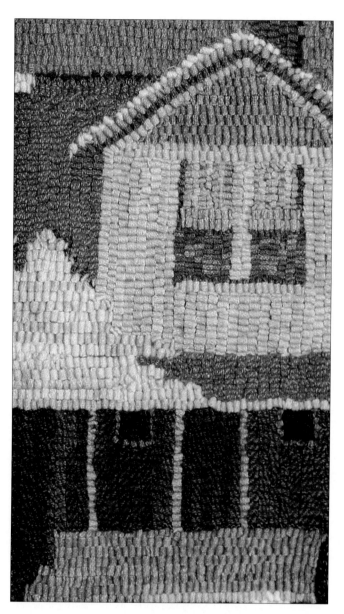

Marilyn Becker has always loved art. She took eight years of private oil painting classes and credits that training in art for her recognition of a photograph that would make a beautiful hooked rug. "My sister gave me a box of Mother's old photos," she says. "I saw the photo of Mom and Dad in the sleigh and just had to hook it."

The story behind the photograph is part of its charm. She explains: "It was November 1928 when this photo was taken. Dad and his step-dad, his mother, and his three sisters had worked hard to break the land and build a large barn and house. Two months before this photo was taken, his step-dad died. Dad inherited the farm. He met Mary, my mom, and they fell in love. Their seven children were born in this house. Later, my sister and husband bought the farm and raised 11 children there. Now their son and his three children own the farm. Five generations have lived there."

Marilyn asked Cathy Stephan to dip dye, spot dye, and pot dye the wool for the rug. The highlights on the snow and the roof of the house are simply washed, off-the-bolt, natural color wool. For a personal touch, Marilyn included some heirloom and special fabrics to add to the genealogy of the piece. She used her father's Pendleton shirt as-is for the shirt in the hooked rug. She also used eyelash yarn to create the fur on her mother's coat. "Mom was so proud of that coat," she said. "It was her first 'store-bought' coat and she purchased it with money she earned waiting on tables at age 14."

For Marilyn, the memories that flooded back as she hooked this piece were what she enjoyed most. "I love the whole thing," she says. "I love the house I grew up in, I love the blankets (I still have one), and I love thinking of Mom and Dad in this sleigh on the farm that they built from scratch."

Marry Me, Mary hangs above the couch in Marilyn's living room, where the sepia colors blend in well with her furniture and stir family memories.

MARILYN BECKER
WAUSAU, WISCONSIN

Marilyn first picked up a hook in 1996, hooked three small pieces, and then didn't touch a rug hooking project again until November 2012 when she was cleaning and found a half-finished chair pad. Marry Me, Mary is the sixth rug hooking she's completed and her first rug to be featured in Celebration.

In the Judges' Words

- *Beautiful technique*
- *Great depth perception*
- *Lovely color palette, sepia with just a dash of color*

Marry Me, Mary, 47" x 37", dyed new and used wool, off-the-bolt wool, and eyelash yarn on rug warp.
Adapted from a family photo, designed with assistance from Cathy Stephan, and hooked by Marilyn Becker, Wausau, Wisconsin, 2013. GALL PHOTO

Martellotti Family Picnic Circa 1928

iz Marino is currently enjoying translating photographs into hooked art. This old family photograph of her husband's family on the way to a picnic near Brooklyn, New York, has always had a special place in her heart.

Her husband's father, Giovanni, is driving the truck while his mother, Ruth (aka Bigga Nonnie), sits on the step of the truck with his Uncle Louis, Uncle Nino, and Esther (aka Little Nonnie). "We always sang a song when we were going to visit: 'Which Nonnie is your favorite Nonnie? I like the Big One. I like the Little One,'" she recalls. "And now I am Mizzy Nonnie to my grandchildren."

Liz dyed two 13-value swatches over Dorr natural and corn and chose two as-is textured wools for the grasses and leaves. She hooked five strips of pure Dorr white into the woman's dress.

Liz found that her emotions over this piece wavered. "Every part, except the sky, was the most challenging thing about this rug," she says. "I was scared every time I started a new motif. I always thought I could not figure out how to do it, but I did! While I was hooking one motif, I would be thinking of the next thing I was going to tackle and visualize in my mind's eye just how I was going to hook it. When it was time, I had worked a lot of my concerns out already."

On completion of the rug, however, Liz can look back and truly say, "I don't think I ever enjoyed hooking anything as much as I enjoyed this piece. I loved the way those boys were and knowing the men they grew into. They do look exactly like themselves as children."

For the border of the rug, Liz used the last $1/2$ yard of her favorite piece of wool, which was given to her by her mentor Maggie McLay. She finished the edges of the rug with whipping. The completed piece hangs in her family room over the mantel.

"When Esther visits us now and looks at the rug, the stories about that day just keep coming," she says. "What a treat to be able to give someone a memory key that opens up the consciousness to those days of her childhood."

LIZ MARINO
SOUTH EGREMONT, MASSACHUSETTS

In 1989, one of Liz's friends watched a show that featured rug hooking and said, "Hey, we should try that!" They did. And Liz has hooked 20 rugs since then. She has won several awards for her work and is pleased to add inclusion in Celebration *to her list.* LISA PRINCE FISHLER

Martellotti Family Picnic Circa 1928, 35¹/₂" x 28¹/₂", #2-, 3-, 4-, and 6-cut wool on rug warp. Adapted by Leonard Feenan from a family photo and hooked by Elizabeth Marino, South Egremont, Massachusetts, 2013. JANE MCWHORTER

In the Judges' Words

- Excellent use of value
- Superb rug with just the right amount of detail
- Depicts texture well

Me Squared

How do you link geometrics and portraits? For Sharon Saknit, it's simply a combination of passion and creativity.

"I love geometrics and creating unexpected visuals within them using tone, texture, and value," she says. "When I shade, I prefer not to use swatches but rather to use miscellaneous pieces of wool in varying colors and gradating values. Most of my current work is done in #6- to 8-cut wool strips."

SHARON SAKNIT
RENTON, WASHINGTON

While staffing a booth at a craft show in 1993, Sharon became intrigued by the artwork of two rug hookers down the aisle. They wisely talked her out of her first dream project—a room-sized floral and scroll rug!—and she's since become a teacher and hooked about 100 rugs. This is her second rug to be featured in Celebration.

Sharon designed this rug by adapting several photos that her brother had taken of her. "I was taking a class on faces from Diane Learmonth and I wanted the challenge of doing a self-portrait," she says. "Color and geometric shapes are really what shaped this rug."

Color planning took place in class. Then Sharon pulled the majority of wool from her worm bag and all her scraps. The only pieces that were dyed specifically for this rug were the multicolored strips that create the main curls in her hair and the dip dye in the wicker.

Sharon found that her face and hair hooked up very quickly, leading her to work on the rug regularly. "I love my eyes and lips. My eyes because they really look like me. My lips because of the variety of wool and colors I used."

But when she got to the neck, shirt, and chair, Sharon lost her motivation and put the rug away for a while. "The wicker chair was the biggest challenge," she says. "First I tried a creative stitch to emulate the wicker in the chair. It was really busy and detracted from the face. I then used regular hooking and dip dyed whites to create a white wicker chair even though the real one was brown. I didn't care for that at all. Next, I dip dyed some browns, which

Me Squared, 25" x 26", #6- and 8-cut wool on monk's cloth. Adapted from family photographs and hooked by Sharon Saknit, Renton, Washington, 2013. MIKE BARNETT

also didn't work. I finally ended up with a combination of the brown dip dyes and an off-the-bolt brown check."

Sharon whipped the edges with yarn colors that matched the loops next to the edge. She used two different-colored strands for an interesting texture and better segue to the next color. The completed rug hangs in her studio and travels with her to rug camps.

In the Judges' Words

- *Great eyes!*
- *Color placement is wonderful*
- *Shape of the piece is fabulous*

Mother

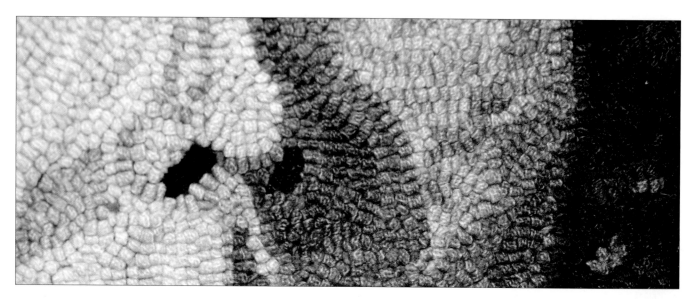

A s Carol Waugh was trying to decide what to hook for a realistic portrait class with Donna Hrkman, she came across a small sepia-toned photograph of her mother inside a small leather graduation booklet. While there was no date on the photo, Carol believes the photo was taken in 1923 upon her mother's graduation from the Red Wing Seminary when she was 20 years old. She decided to hook this photograph into a rug to celebrate her mother's life and as a remembrance that she can pass on to her grandchildren.

Carol purchased much of the wool she needed for the rug after consulting with Donna, but she did dye 10 values of sepia tones from white to the darkest brown using a chestnut brown color over new Dorr white wool. Those colors provided all the tones she needed to hook the border, the background, and the figure of her mother.

Carol worked on the rug intermittently for 11 months and found her mother's hair to be the most challenging feature. She took it out and re-hooked it many times before she achieved the effect she wanted. The hair had to reflect the texture of her mother's hair and serve as a boundary between the vertical background and her mother's face. At the same time, the hair couldn't dominate the composition. Her favorite part of the rug is her mother's eyes. Their detail helps to keep the viewer's focus on the face.

"I learned the importance of looking closely at detail one small area at a time and to hook just exactly what I saw, not what I thought I saw," she says. "I love detail, and learning this technique has helped me to achieve more realistic results in my hooking."

Carol finished the rug with rug tape and whipped edges. She added pockets of rug tape to the top and bottom of the rug in case she decided to hang the rug in the future. Currently, the completed rug is draped over an antique cedar chest that belonged to her husband's mother.

CAROL WAUGH
CHICAGO, ILLINOIS

Carol, a quilter first, became a rug hooker when her friend, Lois Griffith, who enjoyed both quilting and rug hooking, invited her over to make a "mug rug." She immediately picked up another rug hooking project and has hooked 11 projects since that introduction in 2005. Mother is her first rug to appear in Celebration.

In the Judges' Words

- *I marvel at the workmanship*
- *The hooked frame is very effective*
- *Shadows, background, border; wonderful transition*

Mother, 29^1/$_2$" x 40", #3- to 7-cut wool on linen. Adapted from a family photo and hooked by Carol Waugh, Chicago, Illinois, 2012.

Rescue Me

Mary Jean dabbles in just about all things rug hooking. She prefers wider cuts but is open to using whatever cut suits the piece she has on her frame. She likes to hook detailed and realistic patterns, but she also enjoys primitive, fanciful, and offbeat patterns. She loves bright, crazy colors, but she sometimes prefers to work with soft, muted tones. "I am trying to be braver about breaking the rules that I once created for myself," she says.

When she chose to adapt one of Heather Galler's paintings to rug hooking, she was in a bright, fanciful mood. "When I was first introduced to her work, I was awestruck by her vivid and unconventional color plans as well as the way she uses stripes, polka dots, and geometric shapes to make her work interesting, exciting, and fun." She picked the boxer as her subject because she is an active volunteer with New Jersey Boxer Rescue.

Mary Jean followed the color plan that Heather established in the original painting. She used recycled wool, dip-dyed wool, overdyed wool, spot dyes, and as-is wool. "I tend to be a purist; however, I've been pushing myself to incorporate mixed media in my rugs," she says. "Silk sari ribbon comes in an amazing assortment of colors, and I found that the richness and brightness of the colors were perfect complements for the border of this rug." Her border includes one row of colorful ribbon and a second row of black ribbon.

Mary Jean completed this rug in about two years, which is a relatively short time for her. She found the binding to be the most difficult part of the rug, and while she considers the rug finished, she is still not happy with the binding. Her intention is to auction the rug and donate the proceeds in support of the medical costs of the boxers at New Jersey Boxer Rescue.

MARY JEAN WHITELAW
BELLE MEAD, NEW JERSEY

Mary Jean's introduction to rug hooking came from an article in a home and garden magazine and a subsequent visit to Joan Moshimer's rug studio in Kennebunkport, Maine. Since that visit, she's hooked more than 30 pieces, and Rescue Me *is her first piece to be featured in* Celebration.

In the Judges' Words

- *Excellent*
- *Creative use of color*
- *Fun interpretation in textiles of Galler's image*

Rescue Me, 22¹/₂" x 27", #6-, 7-, and 8-cut wool and silk sari ribbon on rug warp. *Adapted with permission from a painting by Heather Galler and hooked by Mary Jean Whitelaw, Belle Mead, New Jersey, 2013.* STACY WHITELAW

Sapphire

Judy Carter hooked this rug as a commission piece to honor Jean Brown's very special pet. Sapphire passed away in 2012 and was a beloved companion and an award-winning show dog. To convey the feeling of a cherished portrait, Judy kept the vertical composition and the posed appearance of the dog in the original photograph by Karen Taylor.

Color planning for this rug was based on the photograph taken by Karen. Judy used all new wool for this rug. She penny dyed the whites and dip dyed the other colors.

Judy created a unique stitch that she calls the wicker basket for this rug. "I have never seen anyone do this in a rug and I developed the idea as I worked on the piece," she says. The woven stitch can be seen on the bench cover on which Sapphire is sitting.

Judy's favorite part of this rug is the dog's eyes. "They were so expressive in the photo, and I wanted to capture that expression," she says. The most challenging part of this rug was hooking the white chest. "Being able to show depth in a large white area can be a challenge. I used the darker areas of penny-dyed wool to show the slight shadows as value changes," she explains.

As she hooked, Judy had to be careful not to allow the busy background to overshadow the focus of the rug. "I learned that a busy background can enhance a piece without detracting from the main part of the rug."

Judy finished the rug with whipping over cording. Because the bench in the rug is woven and not hooked, Judy attached a piece of wool to cover the entire back of the rug to protect the special stitch. The completed rug is currently in the private collection of Jean Brown, Sapphire's owner. "Hooking this piece was special because I know how much this pet meant to Jean," she says. "I'm happy I was able to create a lasting tribute to Sapphire."

JUDY CARTER
WILLOW STREET, PENNSYLVANIA
Judy has hooked 112 rugs since she took a beginner's class in rug hooking in 1983. Sapphire is her 11th rug to be featured in Celebration.

Sapphire, 22" x 26", #3- and 6-cut wool on linen. Adapted, with permission, by Leonard Feenan from a photograph by Karen Taylor (www.pawsinthegarden.com) and hooked by Judy Carter, Willow Street, Pennsylvania, 2013. KAREN TAYLOR

In the Judges' Words

- *Like the surprise of the special technique for the dog's bed*
- *Love her!*
- *Well-done portrait*

The Boy with Far Away Eyes

Maureen Page had hooked two portraits of her daughters, each with a full frontal view. When she decided to hook a third portrait, she chose a photograph that showed a different facial view. The subject in this rug is her 12-year-old grandson, Jacquai. "I made it for my daughter, so I had two tough critics to please."

This photo appealed to Maureen on an emotional level as well. "This picture was taken after his all-star game while the kids were lining up for a team photo," she says. "The sun was setting and colored his eyes green and his cheeks pink. His face is young and childlike, but I can see the muscles in his neck developing into those of a man. It makes me both happy and sad at the same time. He kept his eyes on the ball during the game, but they are focused in the distance now, hence the title."

Maureen planned the colors for this rug based on the many photographs that she had of her grandson. For the skin tones of the face and neck, she used leftover wool from a Tish Murphy facial packet and supplemented the colors with her own swatches. For the eye and the green border, Maureen did a spot dye. She dyed the wool for the hat and shirt in 8-value swatches with jar dyeing. For the background, she pan dyed wool leftovers from her previous projects.

The most challenging aspect of this rug for Maureen was collecting enough color variations for the face and neck. "My daughter is Caucasian, but my grandson is half black, so I needed darker colors than what was included in Tish's kit," she said. "Like an old color TV, I had trouble adjusting the color. But I just kept at it." She also learned that ears weren't as difficult as she thought they would be. "I approached them like everything else: Put the lights and darks where I see them, hook in the direction of the curves, and hope for the best."

The professionally framed piece hangs in Maureen's daughter's living room.

MAUREEN PAGE
MIDDLETOWN, CONNECTICUT

Maureen had always admired hand-hooked rugs, but she didn't have time to try the art until she retired from computer programming in November 2011. Since then she has hooked seven rugs and is thoroughly enjoying her newfound hobby. This is her first rug to be featured in Celebration.

The Boy with Far Away Eyes, 20" x 21¹/₂", #3- and 4-cut wool on monk's cloth. Adapted from family photographs and hooked by Maureen Page, Middletown, Connecticut, 2013. CHARLES FIELDS

In the Judges' Words

- *Value use well done*
- *Fabulous*
- *Great restraint in the color palette and shading*

The Green Woman

DANA PSOINAS
WOODBURY,
NEW YORK

Dana saw Loretta Scena demonstrating rug hooking at a fair and was intrigued enough to sign up for one of Loretta's classes. In the past three years, she's completed eight rugs in several different styles. The Green Woman is her first hooked piece to be featured in Celebration.

Dana Psoinas began *The Green Woman* as a project in Loretta Scena's workshop called Avatars. "I chose the green woman as my avatar because I loved the idea of a goddess of the forest," she says. "This rug really sparked my imagination."

Dana used a mixture of new and recycled wool, wool roving, and ribbon in this rug. Because she was relatively new to rug hooking and hadn't yet developed a large stash, Loretta gave her a bag of wool noodle scraps. Inside were a few skin-colored bundles, which she used for the goddess's face and lips. Other colors for the rug were spot dyed and casserole dyed by Loretta.

The composition of this rug really shows off Dana's favorite part of the rug: the goddess's face. The bright leaves

separate the face from the dark brooding border of the wood, reminding the viewer that the forest often holds danger as well as beauty. The bright fall colors in the leaves are reflected in the goddess's eyes. And the shading of the face reveals a strong light source.

But there isn't just one face in this pattern. Dana also hooked faces in the forest that surrounds the goddess. Two additional faces are camouflaged in the wood border: one on the right of the face and one on the left. "I love to see the expression people have when they realize there are faces in the trees," she says.

Dana worked hard to create a realistic-looking face on the goddess. "It was very important to me that she look realistic—in a powerful goddess sort of way," she says. "I had

The Green Woman, 26¹/₂" x 28¹/₄", #2-, 3-, and 4-cut wool, ribbon, and roving. Adapted with permission from an image by Loretta Scena and hooked by Dana Psoinas, Woodbury, New York, 2013. EILEEN HARITONIDES

to redo some of the face several times to get it just right." She found that stepping away often and taking photos of her progress was helpful and gave her a fresh start when she felt over-whelmed.

Dana framed the finished rug and it hangs in her family room.

The Red Cedar by Emily Carr

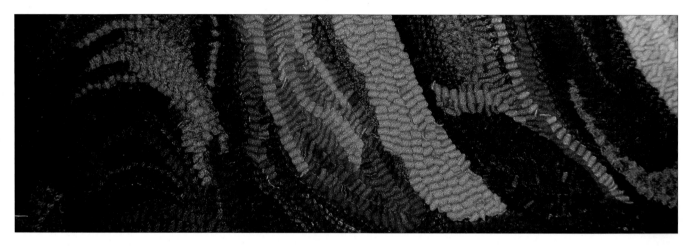

Sunny Runnells first saw this painting in a 2005 calendar from the Vancouver Art Gallery, but it would be another seven years of looking at it until she felt confident enough to hook it. "We live on Vancouver Island surrounded by the forest that artist Emily Carr loved," she says. "Our 60-year-old house is built entirely from red cedar. It felt as if this painting had been made to hang in our house."

Sunny chose the colors for her rug based on the colors that Emily used in the original painting, just making them a little brighter for the hooked piece. She overdyed an abundance of recycled wool for the dark green foliage, and she used spot dyes, dip dyes, and wandering dyes throughout the piece. She found that a few yards of striped wool worked quite well for parts of the tree trunks.

As she worked her way through the hooking process, Sunny discovered that the tree trunk and the roots were her favorite parts to hook. The most difficult area to hook was the foreground. "I drew only a few lines on the backing for this area as it's the most unstructured part of the painting," she says. "I had to compare every row I hooked to the painting to make sure I was keeping it all in perspective."

"I learned the importance of directional hooking to reproduce the brush strokes of this painting," Sunny says. The lines of the hooked rows in each of the elements give the hooked piece depth and movement. The trunks of the trees are hooked vertically, giving them strength and power. The long swirling lines of the trees give the impression of swaying branches and leaves. That movement is echoed on the forest floor in the swelling lines of the earth at the foot of the tree.

To finish the rug, Sunny bound the edge over a cord and whipped it in place. She attached vertical strips of twill tape to the backing to help hold the weight of the rug, and she added horizontal bars of thin wood to keep the rug spread flat. The completed rug hangs on a cedar wall in her living room, which looks out at a red cedar tree.

SUNNY RUNNELLS
LANTZVILLE,
BRITISH COLUMBIA, CANADA

Sunny watched her neighbor hook rugs for years, but it wasn't until she pulled her first loop on her own rug that she know how captivating rug hooking could be. In the past 12 years, she's hooked 25 rugs. The Red Cedar is her second rug to be featured in Celebration.

In the Judges' Words

- *Excellent*
- *Color used to execute depth and movement; amazing*
- *Powerful*

The Red Cedar by Emily Carr, 36" x 56", #8-cut wool on burlap. Adapted with permission from a painting by Emily Carr and hooked by Sunny Runnells, Lantzville, British Columbia, Canada, 2013.

Tiffany Landscape

Jean Ann Kuntz is mesmerized by Tiffany stained-glass windows. After reading the book, *Mr. Tiffany and Me,* she decided to hook a Tiffany-inspired rug. She used a coloring book image as the basis for her design, enlarged it, and altered it to include a more realistic flowing stream. "I'm a West Virginia mountaineer at heart, and I like the movement in the creek," she says.

In the late 1800s, Louis Comfort Tiffany started his artistic journey with paints. At 24, he began experimenting with chemistry and glass-making techniques. His patent for opalescent window glass was registered soon after. True to his artistic roots, this glass-making technique involved combining and manipulating several colors to create a never-before-seen range of hues and three-dimensional effects. His work was unique at that time because the color in the glass came from within the glass itself, not from being painted on the surface of the glass.

To recreate Tiffany's iconic look in wool, Jean Ann relied heavily on dyeing techniques. She color planned the rug to reflect the colors and shading used in a typical Tiffany stained-glass window. Each of the rug's elements reflect the telltale shading, whether it's a single color effect, like in the stream, or several colors that bleed seamlessly one into the other, like in the sky. The wool for the sky was dipdyed by Diana Stoffel. She used both new and recycled wool.

Jean Ann employed a common stained glass technique of bordering each element. In true stained glass, metal boundaries separate the glass colors. Here, Jean Ann hooked lines of black wool around each piece. To emphasize the stained

glass effect, she added black lines to represent several panes of glass being fused together. Directional hooking fills in each element.

For this project, Jean Ann deviated from her usual finishing process of cording and whipping the edges. "I felt it should be treated as a wall hanging," she says. "I hooked a four-inch mitered charcoal-colored frame to match the interior outlining, then framed it all in a black frame." Her completed rug hangs on a wall in her living room where the outdoor light brings it to life.

In the Judges' Words

- *Color choices are so well done*
- *Excellent matching on dips and sky*
- *Good interpretation of stained glass*

JEAN ANN KUNTZ
THE VILLAGES, FLORIDA

When Jean Ann first visited a group of rug hookers at The Villages, she expected to see bits of yarn and latch hooked rugs. She was pleasantly surprised to find primitive rugs, and her mind started spinning with ideas. She has hooked 20 rugs in the past seven years. This is her first rug to be featured in Celebration.

Tiffany Landscape, 36" x 38", *new and recycled wool on rug warp. Adapted from a design by Tiffany of New York as outlined in Dover Coloring Books and hooked by Jean Ann Kuntz, The Villages, Florida, 2013.*

Yesteryear

Roland Nunn chose to adapt an oil painting called *Treasured Memories* by George Kovach. The idea of working through the challenges in hooking a winter twilight scene presented something new and appealing for Roland. "The light involved in a twilight scene is much softer and tends to create more pastel colors than the morning or harsh afternoon light, which leads to much brighter and more vivid colors," he says.

Mr. Kovach's scene had two elements that Roland enjoys hooking: large areas of intricately shaded color and lots of fine detail. To get started, Roland sent a copy of the greeting card that featured the artwork to a transfer service. He color planned the rug based on Mr. Kovach's painting and dyed new wool to match.

"In all of these projects I'm doing, my goal is to hook exactly what I see in all the detail I can," Roland says. "For this rug, I used about 22 different swatches. The key is the use of a parent (base) swatch plus its two transitional companions to create all the subtle variations in color with smooth transitions." Even with all those colors, Roland found matching shadows very difficult, especially those on the snow and the water and those surrounding the steeple.

Other than a few minor variations in the shading of some of the trees, Roland has captured the minutest of detail of the original painting using formulas that he's perfected over 20 years of dyeing. "You really need a complete swatch library to do the kind of work I do," he says. "Having to stop and develop each color as you go would take forever." Roland buys undyed new wool by the bolt and dyes swatches as he needs them for each individual project to keep the amount of wool in his studio to an organized minimum.

Roland rolled the edge over cord and whipped it with wool yarn dyed roughly the same color as the border. He secured the loose edges with rug tape, leaving just enough room to slip pieces of screen molding between the tape and the backing. "The four pieces act like a frame that allows the piece to hang nicely on the wall like a tapestry, but it can still easily be taken apart and rolled up for travel or storage."

ROLAND C. NUNN
ORINDA, CALIFORNIA
Roland remembers his mother hooking rugs, and when he needed a hobby that could be done seated, he thought of her many rugs. To date, he has hooked more than 64 rugs. Yesteryear is his ninth rug to be featured in Celebration.

In the Judges' Words
- *Wonderful job achieving depth on the frozen river*
- *I can smell winter's air*
- *The sky is especially pleasing*

Yesteryear, 35" x 24", #3-cut wool on monk's cloth. Adapted, with permission, from the painting Treasured Memories by George Kovach and hooked by Roland C. Nunn, Orinda, California, 2013. SCOTT McCUE

American Fancy

Jasmine Benjamin lives in a 155-year-old home. Accordingly, the rugs she hooks are made to fit right in. "I strive to hook rugs that look like they've been walked on for a hundred years," she says. "I design my own patterns here and there, but generally I choose from commercially produced patterns. I prefer to hook the less seen or displayed pieces that, of course, can be hooked in an old, faded New England style."

American Fancy caught her eye because the designs of the squares reminded her of antique butter molds. Jasmine customized the rug for her home by choosing the size of the rug and the squares she wanted. "I was able to utilize the size to create a wonderful mirror image of the squares," she says, "which was a smart design technique that allowed me to move my colors around easily."

Keeping all those colors moving was the most difficult aspect of completing the rug, Jasmine says. To start to color plan the rug, Jasmine organized piles of colors for six of the squares with the help of Anne Eastwood. Her mother, Jeanne Benjamin, continued the process. "I moved similar colors around without any repetition of the exact color plan—basically moving color but not using the same piece of wool a dozen times. I had 20 different golds, a dozen blue-teal shades, 17 different reds, and about a dozen greens."

Jasmine used odds and ends and small pieces of wool exclusively so she would have enough color variations. "The quarter- and eighth-yard pieces as well as oddball pieces were perfect for this project," she says. "It felt like I finished a rug after completing each square—instant gratification. I could have kept hooking for another seven feet!"

To finish the rug, Jasmine rolled the linen under and whipped the edges with browns, olives, dark blues, and antique blacks grabbed at random. The completed rug fills the front hall entryway of her home.

JASMINE BENJAMIN
WEST BROOKFIELD, MASSACHUSETTS

Jasmine followed her mom to hooking classes as a 7-year-old kid and couldn't not learn to hook rugs. She attended her first rug camp at age 10. Over the years she has completed an estimated 60 rugs. She is working toward her McGown teacher certification and hopes to follow in her mother's footsteps and teach.

In the Judges' Words

- Very complex color planning; well done
- Good color palette for this huge project
- Holds your interest throughout

American Fancy, 108" x 30", #7- and 8-cut hand-dyed wool on linen. Designed by Eric Sandberg and hooked by Jasmine Benjamin, West Brookfield, Massachusetts, 2013. JEREMIAH BENJAMIN

Jerico

Anne Bond enjoys the diversity inherent in the art of rug hooking, which leads her to explore many styles and techniques. This rug, *Jerico*, gave her the opportunity to work in a primitive style with a dark palette. The rug had caught her eye many times before and she returned to it for this project.

Anne developed a color plan and created new dye formulas specifically for this rug. She dyed 100% off-the-bolt wool in layers to create undertones in the wool that would make the colors glow. The yellows, reds, and oranges that dominate the rug are enhanced by the dark background. Little bits of blue and purple strategically placed inside petals and as outlines for the flowers throughout the design brighten and balance the yellows, oranges, and reds even more.

The double border is Anne's favorite part of this rug. The outside border with the multicolored tongues enhances the color plan and moves the viewer's eye around the rug. The variegated green lines flowing between the elements in the second border adds interest and movement.

Anne found the half circles at the center of the rug to be the most difficult part of the pattern. "They never appeared even," she says. She was never happy with those elements during the five months it took her to complete the rug. But when she was finished and looked at it as one piece, she was quite pleased with the final result.

In hooking *Jerico*, Anne learned that concentrating on contrasts between colors and changing hooking techniques were two keys to creating an eye-catching rug. "The two go hand in hand to make this rug interesting to look at," she says.

Anne finished the rug with cording to match the background of the rug and keep all the colors and elements neatly contained within the rug's space. The completed rug was displayed at and recently sold through a gallery in Indiana.

ANNE BOND
NORTHVILLE, MICHIGAN

Anne owns a rug hooking business called Visions of Ewe. She has hooked 120 rugs since being captivated by a friend's rug in 2001. She has published two books of dye recipes and has created 483 dye formulas for her designer collection. Jerico is her third rug to be featured in Celebration.

In the Judges' Words

- *Incredible use of red on black*
- *Beautifully crafted rug with great color*
- *A nice rug to live with*

Jerico, 8' x 6^1/$_2$', #4- to 9-cut hand-dyed wool on linen.
Designer unknown; hooked by Anne Bond, Northville, Michigan, 2013. LINDA ATKINS

KaBloom

J an Winter enjoys fiber arts in general but finds rug hooking to be a combination of everything she loves about fiberwork. "The repetitive motion of rug hooking is relaxing and meditative, while color planning and designing are mentally stimulating," she says. "It's wonderful to have a hobby that is good both alone and as a sociable pastime with friends."

Jan's friend Rhonda Casper became an integral part of the design of this rug. "This year, I was inspired by artwork of a supernova but wanted to work with a floral form. So I decided to combine the two ideas into one piece. I wanted to show the cycle of life, from death to the exuberant explosion of life in the spring," she says. "Rhonda helped me design the rug using Photoshop. Because of my limited drawing skills, we did it all with simple shapes: twisted, stretched, and repeated to make the flower, leaf, and border forms."

Jan color planned the rug as she hooked. She focused on purple, orange, and pink, cooled off with a little bit of green, and pulled colors from her stash. Eventually, she realized that she would have to buy several values of purple and orange to finish the flames.

"The biggest challenge in hooking this rug was that flame border. I wanted to combine the purple and orange in the border to repeat the flower colors but was unsure if the two color families would meet harmoniously at the points," she says. "I realized that I needed more values to cover each flame point, and I really had to scrounge through my stash boxes to find some darker and lighter textures that would extend my coverage of those points."

In hooking *KaBloom*, Jan learned to be more flexible in her color choices. "I originally wanted a dark border, but the flames got lost. Against my own desires, I had to choose a lighter value and slightly different hue to get the effect I wanted."

JAN WINTER
HOLLYWOOD, CALIFORNIA

Jan's love of quilting led her to rug hooking in 1992 when a fellow quilter shared the book American Hooked and Sewn Rugs. *After attending rug camps for many years, she decided to start her own camp, Cambria Pines Rug Camp, currently run by Gene Shepherd. KaBloom is her 11th rug to be shown in the pages of* Celebration.

In the Judges' Words

- *A delightfully vibrant work*
- *Beautifully hooked*
- *Great colors*

KaBloom, 34" x 24", #6-cut wool on monk's cloth. Designed by Jan Winter and Rhonda Casper, and hooked by Jan Winter, Hollywood, California, 2013. JOE WOLCOTT

Bahamian Sea Life, 66" x 22", #3-, 4- and 6-cut wool on linen. Designed and hooked by Arleen Mauger, Lancaster, Pennsylvania, 2013. NATHAN MAUGER

Beyond Swallowtail, 25" x 39", wool yarn, novelty yarn, and silk sari ribbon on rug warp. Designed and hooked by Karen Miller, Ottawa, Ontario, Canada, 2013.

Cape Shore Crewel, 52" x 38", #3-cut wool on linen. Designed by Pearl McGown and hooked by Helen B. Lynch, Glenmoore, Pennsylvania, 2012. BILL BISHOP/IMPACT XPOZURES

Crazy Horse Quilt II, 60¼" x 39¼", #6- to 8½-cut wool on linen. Designed by Susan Quicksall and hooked by Jo Ann Hendrix, Pasadena, Maryland, 2013. DON DEMENT

February, 36" x 25", #2-, 3-, and 5-cut wool on rug warp. Designed and hooked by Gunda Gamble, Ariss, Ontario, Canada, 2013.

In the Air, 25¼" x 16½", #3-, 4-, and 5-cut hand-dyed and some painted wool on rug warp. Designed and hooked by Lil Quanz, Baden, Ontario, Canada, 2012. KEN QUANZ

Marg's Garden, 36" x 27", hand-dyed wool, fleece, and recycled wool on rug warp. Designed and hooked by Liz Smith, Upper Coverdale, New Brunswick, Canada, 2013.

BLUETTE HIGGINS

Jeff: "Son" and Shadows in Sepia Tone, 10½" by 13½", #3-, 4-, 6-, and 8-cut wool on linen. Designed and hooked by Kathie Meyers, Fayetteville, Georgia, 2012.

My Tree of Life, 28" x 38", #3-, 4-, and 5-cut hand-dyed and repurposed wool on linen. Designed and hooked by Jody Madsen, Calgary, Alberta, Canada, 2013. GARY AND JODY MADSEN

Mimbres, 40" x 28", #4- and 6-cut wool on rug warp. Designed by Jane McGown Flynn and hooked by Phyllis Monjar, Wilmette, Illinois, 2013. HOWARD GORDON

Plato Rupert 3119, 28" x 21", #4- and 6-cut wool on linen. Designed and hooked by Laurie Hannan, Ben Wheeler, Texas, 2013. NOREEN NARTIA

The Stone Fractal, 64" x 43", hand-dyed wool, silk, and sari silk on linen. Designed by Michael Heaphy, Jr., and hooked by Barbara Stone, Nashville, Tennessee, 2013.

Nostalgia, 31½" x 47", #3- to 8-cut wool on monk's cloth. Adapted from a photo from The Outhouse Revisited. *Designed and hooked by Lynn Roth, Rocky Mountain House, Alberta, Canada, 2012.* PAT BATTEN

The Intruder, 35½" x 31", #3- to 6-cut hand-dyed wool on linen. Designed and hooked by Bobbi Tower, Malvern, Pennsylvania, 2012. BILL BISHOP

Storm Coming, 17" x 23", #4-cut Dorr wool on linen. Designed and hooked by Christine Smith, Hillview, Newfoundland, Canada, 2012. EAGEL PHOTO

The Waiting Game, 28" x 34", #6- and 8-cut wool on monk's cloth. Designed and hooked by Wendy Powell, Santa Ynez, California, 2012.

Worm Geometric, 55" x 29", #9-, 9¹/₂-, and 10-cut wool and paisley on linen. Designed by Beverly Conway and hooked by Cynthia Norwood, Austin, Texas, 2012. LARRY NORWOOD

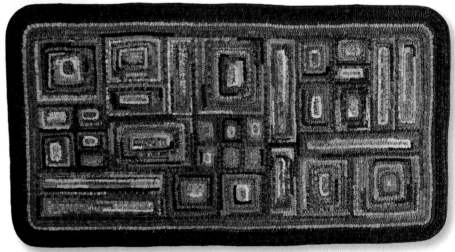

Walking the Dog, 47¹/₂" x 22¹/₂", #4- and 6-cut wool on linen. Designed and hooked by Elizabeth Singleton-Boltik, Lake Wales, Florida, 2012. ELIZABETH KING

R·U·G HOOKING MARKETPLACE

Wide Cut Primitive Rug Hooking

Wide Cut Primitive Rug Hooking is a terrific introduction to these simply designed and popular rugs. Author Wendy Miller writes, "The common bond I feel with the country women of our past is what first attracted me to wide cut, primitive rug hooking." Here you'll find detailed instructions, charming patterns with folk art images, plus tips on using buttons, creating interesting borders, and finishing your rug in a manner that does justice to all of your hard work. Throughout the pages of this comprehensive book, Wendy will also share her tips and techniques on hooking wide cut strips, making new rugs look old, color planning for primitive rugs, hooking details, lettering with wide cuts, and much more! **Price: $24.95***

Prepared to Dye

Have you ever said "I will never dye my wool!" Well, now with Gene Shepherd's new book, you're about to change your mind. This comprehensive guide to dyeing will walk you through the basics of setting up your dye kitchen, prepping your fiber before you dye, dyeing with commercial acid dyes, dyeing without dyes, and so much more. Whether you are a novice or a seasoned dyer, you will use this valuable resource over and over again! Don't miss the opportunity to add this indispensable dyeing resource to your rug hooking library. **Price: $34.95 ***

Scrappy Hooked Rugs

As rug hookers, we all accumulate stashes—those collections of wool left over from previous projects and the wool purchased "because it is so beautiful and I know I'll use it someday!" So how do you design a rug based on your stash of wool? Let Bea Brock, nationally known rug hooking teacher and designer, show you how. You'll have lots of fun in the process! The book is filled with stash-busting ideas for hooking rugs, stash-happy color planning made easy, contemporary scrappy rugs from the experts, and 5 FREE scrappy rug patterns! You'll love the results you can achieve by using this delightful book! **Price: $24.95***

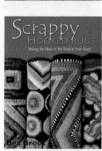

Finishing Hooked Rugs

Don't let finishing your hooked rug be an intimidating process. With *Finishing Hooked Rugs: Favorite Techniques from the Experts,* we've got you covered. This comprehensive book teaches ten different techniques, providing helpful tips and suggestions for professional looking edges. It includes a range of styles from simple whipping to complex combinations of hooking and braiding. Contributors to *Finishing Hooked Rugs* are teachers, designers, and artists well known for their fine work and innovative techniques. This is an absolute must-have for all levels of rug hookers. **Price: $24.95***

You don't want to be without these informative books. Order today!